FOREX FRONTIERS

The Essentials of Currency Trading

Ivan Cavric

Merritt House Publishing Inc.
Toronto, ON

FOREX Frontiers: The Essentials of Currency Trading

ISBN 978-0-9865803-2-1
Copyright © 2010 by Ivan Cavric
Published by:
MERRITT HOUSE PUBLISHING INC.
TORONTO, ON CANADA

www.merritthousemedia.com

Acknowledgements

Forex Frontiers: The Essentials of Currency Trading could not have been written without the support of a number of key people. I truly appreciate the advice, guidance and inspiration from those mentioned here and those I may have accidently left off the list. Several people contributed directly to the success of the book while others contributed indirectly through their research and hands on knowledge of real time Forex trading.

Special thanks goes to the publisher Merritt House Publishing Inc. for making the book available and taking a chance on a new author. In alphabetical order, Terry Allen who assisted me in the writing of the book, the much appreciated assistance and advice of Deanna Cavric head trader for Andover Wellington Partners, Ross Mosquaeda for his dedication in getting all the materials together, Matthew White head trader for Wolsley Finch Inc. for providing real time Forex trading data and Ryan White for the excellent and laborious task in the copyediting of the book. Special thanks to friends and family, - thank you for your support and positive attitude. I give tribute to you all!

Table of Contents

1

Introducing FOREX

Introducing Forex

1.1 – Scope and Purpose

This book is the first of a trilogy. The full set comprises the following titles:

Book 1: FOREX Frontiers: The Essentials of Currency Trading is basically aimed a FOREX novices and introduces the main concepts of this subject in an easy-to-follow style.

Book 2: FOREX Frontiers: Proven Strategies for Success introduces intermediary concepts. In particular, the pros and cons of a number of FOREX trading strategies are discussed in depth.

Book 3: FOREX Frontiers: What the Pros Won't Tell You is intended to help you develop your mindset to that of professional traders by expanding the concepts presented in the first two books. In particular, an introduction to FOREX ideas and strategies for maximizing FOREX earnings are presented.

FOREX is the common abbreviation for the **FOR**eign **EX**change Market which is used by its participants to trade different currency pairs, e.g. EUR/USD and USD/YEN. You can readily ac- cess this vibrant market by employing the facilities and services of one of the many existing Forex brokers.

FOREX is also heavily promoted by extensive marketing campaigns emphasizing how easy it is to make a living, if not a fortune, from trading FOREX. However, it must be realized from the outset that FOREX is a complex subject and trading it successfully is by no means a foregone conclusion.

As you proceed through this book, you will encounter some specialized terms preceding numbers in square brackets. Refer to the reference section at the end of this book for further reading.

This book is intended to advance your FOREX trading experience by acting as a definitive step-by-step guide toward the end of designing successful trading strategies by targeting the most important and commonly cited FOREX concepts. Contained within are straightforward explanations and relevant supporting material such as charts and diagrams.

Chapter 1 explains why FOREX trading is so attractive to so many traders, especially novices. A brief history is provided and common first impressions of FOREX are discussed. The main purposes of this book are also described.

Chapter 2 delves into the mechanics of FOREX trading by explaining what it is and who trades it. Important terminology such as "PIPs" and "spreads" is defined.

Chapter 3 explains why so many novices have difficulty trading FOREX. Unlike other references, this book does not understate the complexities of FOREX trading, but rather lays the foundation for a well-constructed way forward.

Chapter 4 defines the factors to consider when deciding whether FOREX trading is right for you. In this chapter, common obstacles to success and the benefits of FOREX trading are discussed.

Chapter 5 discusses the benefits of having a professional mindset. Examples toward reaching this objective are provided.

Chapter 6 introduces the concepts of designing a simple trading strategy. A number of very popular technical indicators are also described.

Chapter 7 identifies the features of a good FOREX broker. Other useful subjects are also explained, such as how to best use your new trading platform, dealing with volatility and properly trading a demo account.

Chapter 8 deals with the important subjects of risk and money management, in addition to proving advice on best coping with consecutive losses and margin calls. In addition, different types of stop losses and their usefulness for a creating a money management policy are explained.

Chapter 9 introduces the concepts of fundamental analysis. A number of easy to use strategies for trading important news events are also detailed.

Chapter 10 describes the main functions of technical analysis by introducing related strategies designed to facilitate trading under a variety of market conditions.

Chapter 11 explains the principles behind some very popular technical indicators and provides advice on making the best use of these principles.

Chapter 12 explains how to develop your own FOREX trading strategy based on the information provided in the previous chapters.

Chapter 13 presents a real trading strategy that was constructed following the steps presented in Chapter 12. Additionally, field data is analyzed to assess the strategy's performance.

Chapter 14 summarizes the ideas introduced throughout this book and touches on your best way forward.

1.2   Why Does FOREX Attract So Many Novices?

The simple answer to this question is that FOREX affords potential access to a staggering amount of money. As the daily turnover of FOREX is reputed to exceed US$3 trillion per day, the possibility of earning more money than you've ever dreamed is very real. In contrast, the US Stock Market conducts transactions worth only about US$10 billion daily.

FOREX possesses other exciting attributes as well that either greatly exceed those of other trading markets or, in some cases, are unique. These include:

High Levels of both Liquidity and Trading Volumes

Long Trading hours - 24 hours per day except weekends

Global Market with Large Geographical Dispersion

Access to Large Leverage Facilities

Multiple Factors that can Influence Exchange Rates

A Diverse Range of Trading Participants

In addition to the possibility of earning large sums of money in FOREX trading, further attractive benefits may become available by accessing the services of FOREX brokers. Such companies provide very sophisticated trading platforms containing all the tools necessary to trade FOREX. Traders using brokers enjoy features such as extensive leverage; low spreads, especially with the major currency pairs; the ability to trade currencies from charts; hedging; one-click order execution; audible price alerts; training courses and webinars; live support; and free practice accounts.

Many novices are also enticed by numerous adverts, emails promoting FOREX robots, trading courses and strategy guides. Indeed, most of this literature suggests that participants will generate limitless wealth. As a result, it is easy to understand why so many novices are attracted to FOREX.

1.3   A Brief History of FOREX

You may wonder how such an entity, capable of generating such a massive daily turnover, was created. The following is a brief history of FOREX displayed in !Dbular format.

YEAR	EVENT	DESCRIPTION
1900-1920	Early 20th Century	Paper money was introduced.
1929	Stock Market Crash	Dollar status was diminished.
1930	Bank for International Settlements (BIS)	Created to assist countries with balance of payment problems.
1931	Great Depression	Large reduction in global trading.
World War II	British Pound Status	USD replaces GBP as dominant currency
1944	Bretton Woods Conference	Debated the financial future of the post-war world introducing tighter controls on currency values. USD becomes the World's reserve currency.
1957	Birth of EEC	European Economic Community was born.
1967	IMF meeting in Rio de Janeiro	Special Drawing Rights were created to supplement the existing reserve assets.
1971-1972	The Smithsonian Agreement (SA) and European Joint Float (EJF)	SA increased Currencies Movements relative to the US dollar. EJf was created to control currency fluctuations for its members.
1973	SA and EJF	Both systems collapsed because of heavy market pressure.
1978-1979	International Monetary Fund (IMF) and European Monetary System (EMS)	IMF authorized free currency floating. EMS was established.
1999	EURO	The Euro was introduced within the EEC.
2002	The Single Currency	Euro replaces all national currencies within the EEC on 1st January 2002.

FOREX has witnessed amazing volume growth since currencies were permitted to float against each other. This market had a daily turnover of US$5 billion in 1977, which has now increased to US$3 trillion per day.

There have been a number of major contributing factors to this staggering growth, including business internationalization, traders' sophistication, corporate interest increases, telecommunications developments and interest rate volatility.

1.4   Early Misconceptions

Before deciding to trade FOREX, one must dispense of any over-optimistic preconceived ideas and focus on reality. For instance, statistics indicate that 95% of all FOREX novices squander their entire initial equity within a couple of months from startup.

It may also be unnerving to discover that, in practice, less than 5% of all traders even make a living from trading FOREX. Consequently, it is crucial to identify methods that will aid in the separation of marketing hype from reality. Indeed, FOREX is difficult to trade successfully and many are misled into believing otherwise. You must proceed with caution and take the time to find your "FOREX legs" before you throw your hard-earned money into this activity.

For example, while FOREX's gigantic daily turnover is impressive, it shouldn't be a preoccupation. Rather, this turnover should be analyzed from a different perspective. As opposed to staring boggled-eyed at these enormous cash amounts, one should make efforts to determine how such massive sums can be generated in the first place. The reality is that FOREX involves the trading activities of a staggering number of global market participants. In addition, some participants are corporations and governments who possess extensive budgets and varying agendas. These organizations can activate substantial currency movements by themselves, with no prior warning to other FOREX participants.

It is also worth noting that the massive FOREX daily turnover can generate the power to produce very intricate and complex trading formations that even the best experts have difficulty predicting. As such, substantially improving what we will call "FOREX awareness" is integral to controlling the intense power of FOREX to a point that it can be traded successfully.

Note that your own fiscal reserves and trading experience may not approach those of FOREX experts. Consequently, psychological preparation is needed for the war ahead, or you will find yourself the equivalent of a leaf being blown wildly in a hurricane.

Keeping in mind the vast number of novices who fail miserably at FOREX trading, it should come as no surprise that preserving your initial equity is extremely important. If one is to prosper from FOREX trading, it shouldn't be thought of as a "get rich quick" scheme. As with any activity involving large sums of money, FOREX trading should be treated in a business-like manner. This book teaches this all-important skill.

Consider for a moment that FOREX experts exhibit a completely different trading psychology from beginners. The following chapters provide detailed information on how these professionals have enhanced their mindsets so that they are in complete control of their FOREX futures. In addition, as you will quickly realize that no other source or individual will pro- vide you with instant success, you will begin to take measures to ensure that all your educational and training needs are fully met.

If anything, *FOREX Frontiers: The Essentials of Currency Trading* should emphatically demonstrate that one's mindset can be successfully elevated to that of an expert if the proper steps are followed. Of course, achieving such a valuable state of mind requires a time commitment on par with the rewards. However, this commitment is essential to ensure success in the dynamic world of FOREX trading.

2

The FOREX Market Explained

The FOREX Market Explained

2.1 – FOREX Fundamentals

FOREX [1] is both the most liquid and the largest financial market in the world. Large fiscal institutions such as businesses, governments, banks, currency speculators, and individuals use FOREX to exchange and trade currencies. FOREX generates a daily turnover that is in excess of US$3 trillion and is mainly used to advance global trade and investment. FOREX involves the simultaneous selling of one currency and the buying of another, thereby functioning to expedite international trade.

Currencies bought and sold on FOREX are, for all intents and purposes, commodities. Consequently, the purchase of a particular country's currency is, in fact, an investment in the economy of that country. When that country posts improving economic data, the value of its currency will in turn raise in relation to that of other countries' currencies. Under such circumstances, the FOREX trader would record a profit.

It should be understood that two trades are actually taking place when one selects a currency pair. For example, choosing the Australian Dollar/US Dollar (AUD/USD) combination means that one would be buying the AUD whilst selling the USD. This action constitutes a commercial relationship among the trader and the two currencies—an important revelation if one is to fully grasp and the intricacies inherent in the relationship between the two currencies.

FOREX operates 24 hours a day, from Sunday at 5:00 pm EST to Friday at 4:00 pm EST and is the world's most traded market. Each trading day, FOREX commences in Sydney and then circulates around the world, passing through Tokyo, London and New York. During this time, one has the opportunity to trade changes in currency movements. FOREX may be thought of as a huge melting pot, reacting almost instantaneously to international events. In addition, FOREX exists because of the constant need to trade foreign cur- rencies against each other and hedge risk, thereby making international trade possible.

As currencies move against each other in FOREX in real time, one can profit from these changes by correctly predicting which currencies will increase in value against others. To do so, one must first purchase their chosen currency and then sell it after it appreciates in value against the other currency. It is important to be aware that the time required for a profit to be achieved could range from a very short period to a very long one. For example, the following USD/CAD chart shows a basic but nonetheless important principle of FOREX trading: One needs to buy the USD low and sell it high in order to achieve a profit.

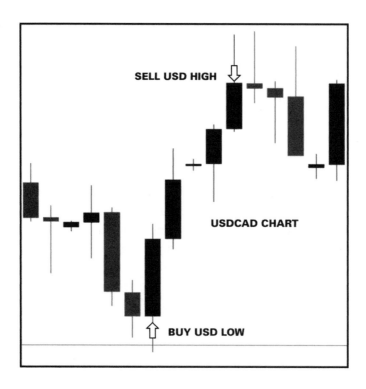

The majority of FOREX trades involve the biggest and most liquid currencies, often termed the "Majors" [2]. These currencies include the USD, Japanese Yen (YEN, or JPY), Euro (EUR), British Pound (GBP), Swiss Franc (CHF), Canadian Dollar (CAD) and AUD. As shown in the diagram below, more than 85% of all FOREX currency transactions are centered on these major currency pairs (i.e., AUD/USD, USD/CAD, USD/CHF, GBP/USD, USD/YEN and EUR/USD).

As currencies are traded in pairs, one can profit from ex-change rate moves by purchasing a currency that is anticipated to strengthen against another. For example, if it is determined that the EURO (EUR) will increase in value against the dollar (USD), then purchasing the EUR/USD combination may generate a profit.

You can invest in FOREX trading by using borrowed capital sup- plied by your FOREX broker. This is termed margin trading and allows you to utilize between 0.5 and 4 percent of your own equity to support a large financial position. Such a facility will allow you to leverage [3] your trading positions.

FOREX can be traded using lots. A standard lot is worth US$100,000. Some brokers will allow traders to use smaller units called mini-lots and micro-lots. As one currency will always be strengthening against another, one does not need to wait for a bullish market to gain profit. One of FOREX's most significant attributes is that it is constantly generating opportunities for profits.

2.2 – Who Trades FOREX?

All FOREX transactions are performed on the interbank market [4] or OTC (over the counter) via phone or electronic networks because it does not utilize a centralized exchange. FOREX turnover is generated by two main trading sources. The first is foreign trade produced on the part of organizations buying and selling their products in foreign countries and the conversion of foreign sales into domestic currency.

The organizations in this trading group include governments, companies (exporters and importers) and some investors who have foreign exchange exposure. Their profits can be strongly influenced by the oscillations between their domestic currencies and the foreign currencies of their overseas investment or business partners. These activities represent only 5 percent of total FOREX turnover.

The other 95 percent of FOREX turnover is generated by the speculation trade, which consists of transactions made for pure profit. In the speculation trade, funds, corporations and banks create artificial rate exposure in order to profit from the price movements of currency pairs. Consequently, the majority of FOREX trading is purely speculative. Only a small percentage of this market's activity is the result of the fundamental currency conversion needs of governments and companies.

2.3 – Major FOREX Influences

There are several major factors that influence the demand and supply of any given currency pair. These factors are market psychology, economic considerations and political events.

Market psychology can affect FOREX in the following ways:

1. Disturbing international developments can produce risk

aversion [5], resulting in traders seeking safe haven investments.

2. The "buy the rumor, sell the fact" maxim can influence major events before they have occurred. Quite often under these circumstances, the market then reacts in the opposite way after the anticipated event happens.

3. The posting of important economic data can directly influence market psychology, producing substantial short-term currency fluctuations.

Examples of market psychological factors include, but are not limited to, government budget deficits or surpluses, balance-of-trade levels and trends, inflation levels and trends, economic growth and the productivity of an economy. You can consult the Global Economic Calendar [6] to find the specific times and dates of every major economic data release.

The economic factors that affect FOREX include policy making and economic developments. For instance, the financial policies of a nation can directly impact the interest rates of its central banks, thereby influencing the supply and cost of its money.

Internal, regional and international political events can also have a significant impact on the movements of currency pairs. For instance, if a country is plagued by instability and political uprisings, such developments can negatively influence its economy and, subsequently, the performance of its currency. Such events can powerful enough to positively or negatively impact the currencies of other countries.

2.4 – Some Basic FOREX Rules

Before one commences trading, there are a number of rules for trading currency pairs that should be considered:

- The first currency that is listed in a pair is termed the base currency.

- The second currency is denoted as the counter or quote currency.

- Currencies are always traded in pairs. For instance, the EUR/ USD combination represents the current quoted price for the Euro versus the US Dollar. If the EUR/USD price is displayed at 1.3950, then a trader can exchange US$1.3950 for every one Euro.

- As the US Dollar is the world's reserve currency, it is normally the base currency of most of the major currency pairs.

- When a currency pair rises in value, this means that the base currency has increased in value whilst the counter has dropped. For example, if the EUR/USD price rises to 1.4100, a trader will be able to exchange US$1.4100 for every one Euro.

2.5 - Most Traded Currencies

Some currencies are traded more heavily than others. The following table shows the most popular currencies exchanged on FOREX.

Currency	ISO Code	% Daily Share
United States Dollar	USD $	86%
Euros	EUR €	37%
Japanese Yen	JPY ¥	17%
Pound Sterling	GBP £	15%
Swiss Franc	CHF Fr	7%
Australian Dollar	AUD $	7%
Canadian Dollar	CAD $	4%

FOREX traders often use abbreviations or nicknames when referring to currency pairs. The following table defines the terms that are most commonly used, although there are many other abbreviations and nicknames applied to currency pairs.

Currency Pair	Nickname
AUD/USD	AUSSIE
USD/CAD	BEAVER
USD/JPY	GOPHER
USD/CHF	SWISSY
USD/CAD	LOONIE
NZD/USD	KIWI
GBP/JPY	GEPPY
EUR/USD	EURO

It should be apparent from the tables above that most of the major currency pairs involve the US Dollar. In addition, it should be noted that the major currencies are identified by using their ISO codes as listed above. There are also many other cross currency pairs, such as EUR/GBP, GBP/YEN, EUR/YEN, EUR/CHF and AUD/YEN.

It is important to realize that the above currency pairs are still calculated using USD pairs although they are quoted independently. One can use crosses to help trade other currency pairs that do not include the US Dollar.

2.6 – Introducing PIPs

PIP is the abbreviation for Percentage in Points and represents the smallest price unit of a FOREX currency that can be changed. For example, when the value of the EUR/USD pair rises by one PIP, then the quote will move from 1.4100 to 1.4101. An important guideline recommends measuring your FOREX trading performance in PIPs as opposed to monetary values.

An example of a PIP movement using the EUR/USD currency pair is as follows: Assume that the EUR/USD value is quoted at 1.3920. Should the pair climb to 1.3938, then it would have increased in value by 18 PIPs.

2.7 – Gaining Access to FOREX

FOREX can be traded by using a number of different pricing levels. The interbank market is the highest level of access but is reserved for major investors such as central banks, corporations, hedge funds and other large financial institutions.

Since the arrival of the Internet, the general public has been able to access FOREX trading by using the facilities supplied by FOREX brokers. Fundamentally, that there are two types of brokers: Market makers [7] utilize dealer desks whilst the second group employs Electronic Communication Networks (ECNs) [8]. Each type of broker has its pros and cons.

Market makers are the more common type of broker, operating as intermediaries to the interbank market. Market makers do not normally provide direct access to the FOREX market, but rather trade large blocks of currency on the interbank market that they then allocate into smaller units for their clients.

ECNs can offer you direct access to the interbank market by connecting you to multiple banking entities that offer competitive price quotes for currency pairs. ECNs and market makers have many differences:

1. ECNs can provide you with real-time quotes for currency pairs from many sources, but their prices will not be as stable as those supplied by market makers.

2. ECNs can generate more competitive prices and spreads because of multi-sourcing.

3. As ECN brokers will not be competing against you, they have no vested interest in trade results. Consequently, they have no reason to apply unethical price manipulation tactics.

2.8 – Types of FOREX Orders

One can open FOREX trading positions by using many types of orders:

1. Entry limit orders can be used to open a new FOREX position to sell if it has been determined that price will reverse direction at the level of the order. For example, assume that the EUR/USD pair is rising and is presently quoted at 1.3910. However, in anticipation that it will fall you set an Entry Limit Order at 1.3880. Should the EUR/ USD drop to 1.3880, your current open position will be sold and closed.

2. Entry Orders can be activated to open a position once one's chosen currency pair attains a pre-determined price value. For example, assume that the EUR/USD is rising and has a current value of 1.4050. If it is expected that this pair will rise even further, an Entry Order can be set at 1.4100. A new position will be opened if the EURUSD achieves 1.4100.

3. To activate a new position immediately at the best available current price, one may use a market order. For example, if the EUR/USD presently trades at 1.3980, a market order will allow you to open a new position at this price

2.9 – The Implications of FOREX Spreads

The difference between the ask price and bid price of a currency pair is termed the spread [9]. When one purchases the base currency of a pair, the price is termed the bid price. The bid price is positioned on the left in currency pair quotes. For example, in the diagram below, the USD/CHF pair is 0.9768/73. In this case, your bid price is 0.9768.

Similarly, currency may be bought at its ask price, which appears on the right of a currency pair's quote. For example, in the above diagram, the ask price for the EUR/USD pair is 1.3955.

↑ EURUSD	1.3952	1.3955
↑ USDCHF	0.9768	0.9773
↓ GBPUSD	1.5678	1.5684
↓ USDJPY	81.35	81.40
↓ USDCAD	1.0255	1.0262
↓ NZDUSD	0.7464	0.7470

The spread between the bid and ask prices represents a broker's commission. For example, if one buys the EUR/USD pair at 1.3955, it would only be worth 1.3952 if it is sold immediately afterwards. This represents an instant loss of 3 PIPs, which is the broker's spread commission. It is apparent from this example that seeking brokers offering the lowest spreads possible is extremely important. This is because one must gain the spread to simply break even for every position opened.

3

Why Do So Many FOREX Novices Fail?

Why Do So Many FOREX Novices Fail?

3.1 – Identifying Limitations

What, in fact, does go so wrong for so many FOREX beginners? Some insights and possible answers to this question may be obtained by researching the facilities and information released by large FOREX brokers [10]. It should be noted that the majority of beginners eventually depend on such data as their main method for trading once they realize the limits of their own FOREX abilities.

FOREX brokers provide their clients with very comprehensive and well-researched advice and notifications about when the entry and exit points of all the major currency pairs occur. These guidelines generally provide good results because FOREX brokers benefit greatly from the success of their clients. The quality of a broker's advice is usually high because it is produced by a team of FOREX experts utilizing the following concepts:

1. The identification of achievable targets
2. Advised actions at each encountered intermediate level depending on the market's current conditions
3. Money and risk management
4. Findings from expertly deployed statistical trading techniques
5. Historical back testing
6. Pivot points [36] to identify key support, resistance, and intermediate levels
7. Stop strategies to reduce risks and losses
8. Regular updates as your live trades progress

Of course, on the surface the production of such information sounds great, especially given light of the fact that most FOREX brokers can provide proof that they really do achieve profits from their own recommendations over the long haul. However, please note that much can go wrong if you mindlessly follow their advice without sufficient planning. To illustrate why, consider the following example.

Imagine your FOREX broker has advised you to open a new position in order to trade a currency pair with a 100 PIP target. At first sight this may appear to have the potential to be a winning trade. However, note that you may need to maintain your position open for many hours before achieving the planned profit.

Be aware that FOREX can generate sudden and vicious price movements very quickly and without warning to traders. Should such an event happen, you could be caught off guard despite the fact that your FOREX broker is supplying you constantly with updates.

Under such circumstances, the FOREX broker could very well react to this sudden development with a quick and appropriate response because brokers possess an experienced staff and large supercomputers that can constantly monitor each trade using numerous analytical tools and techniques. In contrast, you will almost certainly not have these types of advantages at your disposal.

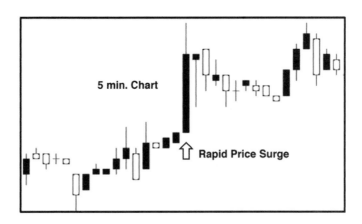

5 min. Chart

Rapid Price Surge

A look at historical and statistical evidence will reveal that even the best FOREX experts still open positions that fail. However, they are more able to devise strategies that will minimize their losses by utilizing well-developed risk and money management concepts [11]. In contrast, a novice may not possess such skills and knowledge, and certainly doesn't have the ability to monitor movements 24 hours a day.

It should also be understood that a FOREX broker may not be able to provide important updates quickly enough. This task can sometimes be quite daunting in real time, despite the size of a broker's staff. You can never rely solely on the facilities of third parties. Without exception, you must always be your first line of defense when it comes to FOREX trading.

Another important point to consider is that brokers may have comparatively larger budgets than you, allowing them to endure a number of consecutive losses. For instance, larger equities may allow brokers to trade by risking much less per open position than is possible for the novice trader.

In conclusion, the following comparison will quickly explain why novice traders may have more initial problems trading FOREX than a broker, company or larger, more experienced trader.

1. Professional traders may have a highly experienced and qualified staff that is proficient in all concepts related to FOREX trading, economics, statistical mathematics and any number of other specialties.

2. Supercomputer facilities at the disposal of professional traders are able to track many FOREX currently pairs concurrently using multiple statistical tools.

3. Professional traders have access to large libraries of historical FOREX data for each currency pair.

4. Professional traders are capable of tracking live positions 24 hours a day and reacting to any new developments

swiftly and appropriately.

5. Professional traders have large budgets that allow them to endure the occasional loss.

A novice trader's resources may be restricted for the following reasons:

1. A novice has very limited FOREX experience and training.
2. A novice's trading facility is generally a standard desktop PC.
3. A novice does not have the benefit of a large, experienced staff.
4. The need for sleep precludes the possibility of tracking FOREX movements 24 hours a day.
5. A novice's equity may be very limited, making consecutive losses a serious issue.
6. A novice is dependent on expert advice to inform relating to the significance of each new FOREX development.

From the above, it should be apparent that novices do not possess the resources to trade FOREX in the same way as a company or broker. Can you still succeed and make profits? Yes, but you will need to learn how to devise a FOREX trading strategy that is based on your specific limitations when it comes to experience and resources. This book will clearly show you how to achieve this objective in well- defined steps.

3.2 – Problems Related to Initial FOREX Impressions

Many are attracted to FOREX trading after an intense exposure to the massive amount of marketing literature and publicity surrounding this subject. It's no wonder that the many attractive attributes of FOREX can readily seduce would-be traders into thinking that it is an excellent possibility for a new business.

However, novices who have already started to trade may conclude that they have bitten off more than they can chew. A recent survey probed the thinking habits of novice FOREX traders and discovered the following unrealistic expectations:

1. Many novices initially thought that all they had to do was purchase or acquire a FOREX automated solution or trading strategy to achieve success. Many beginners even believe that they do not need to make any real effort themselves to learn how to trade FOREX properly.

2. Did you know that you must utilize good risk and money management concepts as a top priority in order to provide the maxi- mum protection for your equity?

3. Many novices seek excitement and thrills by planning to trade a large number of positions daily, believing that by doing so they have a greater chance to generate profits more quickly.

4. Do you have difficulty accepting losses and do not realize that even experts do not win every trade?

5. Novices also tend to jump from one FOREX strategy to the next without persevering for any serious length of time.

6. Do you think that 80% of your FOREX trades will be outright winners?

Once one acquires a minimum amount of experience at trading FOREX, it will become apparent that the above list is fantasy. The only real use the above misconceptions provide is to point out that many beginners think that FOREX trading is a way to instant riches that requires little effort. Indeed, such naïve ideas will result in nothing more than rapid and significant financial losses.

In contrast, the following guidelines make up a good FOREX strategy. By studying them, you will begin to appreciate the type of thinking that must be developed in order to successfully trade FOREX.

1. Open new positions that will last for about two to six days on average.
2. Aim to action just one high-quality trade a day.
3. Aim to trade a maximum of thirty positions per month.
4. The targeted profit should not exceed 100 PIPs at maximum, although you should aim to average 20 PIPs per trade.
5. Target profits of 300 PIPs a month and 3000 PIPs annually.
6. Evaluate the performance of your trading strategy on a regular basis.
7. Implement a strategy that will restrict risk exposure to a maximum of two percent of your entire equity per trade.\

3.3 - Making Quality Decisions Consistently

To trade FOREX successfully, one must develop a psychology that will allow for the consistent generation of quality decisions. Acquiring this skill is very important in order to learn how to react swiftly and appropriately to the new developments that constantly arise in the world of FOREX trading.

One simply does not have the luxury of distraction. Avoid gut feelings and emotions as they will negatively influence trading decisions.

It is preferable to detach oneself from surrounding stimuli as a means of focusing on trading in a professional manner. For example, good money management skills are keys to avoiding overtrading and consequently exposing your account to margin calls [23]. A good grounding in money management skills can minimize stress levels and result in a much calmer attitude when trading. Avoiding stress puts the novice trader in a better position to make informed, fact-based decisions.

On the other hand, failure to introduce measures that neutralize margin calls will result in worry about whether open positions are sustainable. Under such circumstances, agitation and distraction tend to set in. Make no mistake, margin calls are distressing events that can cause significant psychological trauma if the proper precautions aren't taken.

Without good money management skills, it's very difficult to consistently make sound trading decisions. A novice trader must also contend with a continual influx of new FOREX developments in addition to dealing with positions that are already open. It should be obvious that trading FOREX is an activity that is capable of producing high stress levels.

FOREX is influenced by so many different factors that it is almost impossible to initially master all of them. For instance, one would have to become an economic expert to analyze every fundamental consideration and learn all the important aspects of technical analysis.

To successfully trade FOREX, an extremely large amount of new information must be learned in a very short period of time. As such, this book encourages a focus on developing a trading strategy in clearly defined steps. Once you have achieved this objective, it's time to learn techniques that can provide maximum protection for your equity. This important process will go a long way toward reducing the stress related to potential financial losses.

3.4 – FOREX Trading Produces Stress

FOREX is a complex subject, largely because it is influenced by multiple variables. For example, FOREX has a daily turnover that is in the region of US$3 trillion. This large sum of money entices many novices into trying their luck at trading FOREX because they think that they have good chances of earning just a portion of this massive amount. However, this is the wrong way to proceed. Instead, one should concentrate on determining how such a gigantic sum could be produced in the first place.

Try to imagine what on this planet could produce such a flow of money. This exercise will aid in the adoption of better methods of trading. Any cursory investigation of this topic would result in the knowledge that FOREX generates price movements as a result of the currency transactions actioned by a massive number of traders worldwide, each possessing their own agenda.

This is why FOREX is such a vibrant environment in which to work, and why it is capable of generating high volatility [12] and complex price patterns. Furthermore, FOREX possesses a very high speed of operation that can produce price movements of hundreds of PIPs in just minutes.

As a result of the above complexities, one should develop an objective understanding of the nature of FOREX, thereby gaining foreknowledge of many common problems that may arise during trading. It is much easier to take the necessary actions to preserve your equity once a clear understanding of FOREX itself is developed.

It's important that analytical skills not become blurred by reacting to gut feelings. A string of losses shouldn't result in frustration and despair. Such emotions will only derail overall objectives. Conversely, a series of consequent wins and the resultant elation should not result in overconfidence and greed. You must learn to trade with a cold detachment.

This book advocates a professional mindset as a means of trading consistently and with discipline. This manner of thinking effectively optimizes your chances of making consistent, quality decisions. Understand that FOREX requires nothing less than the above attitude because of the vast number trading situations it can generate. If you consistently expose yourself to trading situations that require rapid decisions, it can be mentally draining.

Finally, it should be reiterated that one's level of concentration must be maintained while trading FOREX. If you allow your whims free reign, it will be that much more difficult to make quick, accurate decisions when necessary. Any study of FOREX trading statistics and historical records will reveal that such an approach will only lead to significant financial losses. This book is intended to show how a novice trader may overcome these problems.

4

Successful FOREX Trading

Successful FOREX Trading

The last chapter identified reasons why so many novices fail at FOREX trading. is the discussions in Chapter 3 were not meant to dissuade you from becoming a FOREX trader, but were rather intended to help in the development of a sound trading approach from the outset. This chapter explains the benefits of becoming a FOREX trader.

4.1 – You Must Have Realistic Objectives

If one is prepared to adopt the right attitude, then trading FOREX trading can be a very profitable activity. Put simply, above average returns are possible if tone learns how to control the above average risks associated with the profession.

For instance, learning how to trade like FOREX experts is certainly an advantage because, as can be expected, these experts make significantly greater profits than beginners. A good place to start is to understand why expert FOREX traders profit from their activities. To do this, one must understand the psychology of novices when they are first confronted by the intimidating FOREX environment. Most of them are badly prepared because they were likely attracted to FOREX by all the intense marketing campaigns and publicity surrounding it.

As such, a novice's initial objectives would be completely unrealistic in that they would think that FOREX is a "get rich quick" scheme with the potential for easy profit. Even if they do have a trading strategy, it will most certainly be weak. Many novices do not understand that they will not be able to win all of their positions. They fail to realize that even experts experience losses and that the best they can hope for is to engage in more profitable trades than they do losing ones.

Beginners also have minimum money and risk management awareness; they consistently overtrade by risking far more than they can afford to lose. Generally, novices do not realize the importance of restricting their risk per trade to a maximum of 2 percent of their total equity. In reality, only a small proportion of FOREX traders are successful. Most novices fail because of one or more of the following reasons:

1. Novices do not know how to use demo trading properly.

2. Likewise, beginners do not understand how to design a well-tested FOREX trading strategy.

3. Novices have minimum money management skills and tend to overtrade, risking constant margin calls.

4. They have not developed a robust trading psychology that prevents their emotions from influencing their trading decisions.

5. Many novices approach FOREX with a gambler's mindset as opposed to treating it very seriously.

6. They commence trading with real money before they have developed and fully tested a FOREX trading strategy using a demo account.

7. Beginners attempt to trade multiple currency pairs at the same time before they have achieved a profitable track record with just one currency pair.

Harboring any of the attitudes listed above will result in problems when trading FOREX. Can one take steps to overcome these problems and validate the decision to become a FOREX trader? Yes, but a more realistic approach is required.

This book will help you develop just such an approach by mapping out an easy-to-follow and methodical plan that will minimize risks and maximize profits even before risking real money. Think of a novice FOREX trader as someone training to become a doctor or a lawyer. These skills do no evolve overnight. A would-be FOREX trader must study and adopt a more scientific and business-like approach.

For instance, this book will develop the basics of a proven trading strategy that will enable novices to achieve this objective. The methodology entails advancing a low risk trading configuration to a high risk configuration using a well-tested, iterative process. The first step in this process is to develop a trading strategy with specific configuration settings.

The goal is to use the trading strategy developed herein to detect trends. This will maximize profits while avoiding false price blips. of the concept of technical analysis [13] will also be explained. Technical analysis aids in the identification of the best functions to be included in a trading strategy. Later chapters will address these topics in more detail.

This book will provide clear instructions on how to commence trading by creating a demo trading baseline that can be used to compare all future strategy updates. For example, you will be advised to configure your trading strategy to low risk using the following settings: Trade one lot only, risk a maximum of 2 percent of your total margin per trade, trade only one currency pair at a time and have only one live position active at any one time.

It is important to understand that there is a significant difference between risking 2 percent and 10 percent of your total equity per trade. Ten trades, risking only 2 percent of your total equity per trade, would result in a loss of 17 percent of the total balance if every trade were a loss. Under the same conditions, risking 10 percent on the same number of trades would produce losses in excess of 60 percent.

Obviously, the first case provides much better protection

in terms of equity. Utilizing this type of strategy will significantly extend your survival while trading FOREX. Indeed, an important concept to appreciate is that FOREX experts are great survivors first and big earners second.

Another important concept explained in this book is how to calculate the expectancy value [14] of a given trading strategy by utilizing a statistical batch of at least 50 trades. The expectancy value is a statistical parameter that increases in accuracy as the number of trades, included in its calculation, rises.

This parameter can then be used to determine if a trading strategy really does make profits. In addition, expectancy values will assist you in selecting sound money management strategies.

The expectancy value projects the average profit that a trader can expect to achieve for every US$1 risked over the long haul. A negative value represents a potential loss while a positive one implies profits. Comparing the expectancy values of different trading strategies will enable quantitative comparisons of their historical performances. In fact, this is one of the many optimum methods used to measure and then adjust a strategy for better performance.

4.2 – A Good FOREX Education is Vital

Statistical analysis shows that less that 5 percent of all FOREX traders are successful. Many experts indicate that one of the most important keys to success is the correct choice of education. Consequently, in order to validate your decision to become a FOREX trader, it is important that this very important step not be omitted.

What composes a good FOREX education? Learning techniques that will help preserve equity in order to help ensure your survival in the world of FOREX trading is a top priority. Other important FOREX topics, such as how to design a FOREX trading strategy, money management and risk control, are also necessary. This book will save you extensive amounts of time by focusing on the key subjects required to trade FOREX successfully.

It is extremely important that a working understanding of all the topics contained within this book is developed. Indeed, becoming familiar with the strategies herein is surely a better option than gambling mindlessly on the complexities of FOREX. Quality courses are also available that will add to the advice that this book offers. It should be noted that while many educational websites simply cover FOREX basics, this book provides comprehensive coverage that few, if any, websites can hope to match.

The key to successfully trading FOREX is finding quality information that will help develop your trading psychology. Confidence levels, discipline and perseverance then necessarily increase—all of which are essential characteristics of successful FOREX traders. The first step is evaluating your present level of FOREX education in order to develop a baseline to judge progress.

A good education will explain how to create a FOREX trading strategy in installments. Choose one that explains a strategy that really works and produces profits. This objective can be achieved by studying reviews and discussions on one or more of the many available FOREX forums and blogs.

A novice can definitely make great steps toward acquiring increased FOREX profits by developing the right psychology through education. It is important to learn how to take well-calculated risks to avoid severe problems relating to the extreme volatility associated with trading FOREX. A comprehensive FOREX education must not be restricted to learning how tools and training plat- forms perform, but must also focus on the novice's trading psychology.

FOREX techniques and tools are, of course, important, but it is the correct usage of them over the long haul that will determine how successful a FOREX trader will become. Developing the correct attitudes will take some time, but once achieved, you will be in complete control of your trading and not dependent on any particular source. Again, this book contains all the information to help you achieve these goals and set you firmly on your path to success.

Fundamentally, education is the key to trading like an expert. To help explain this point, below is a comparison between the ways a novice thinks and the ways an expert thinks.

1. Novices exhibit a psychology that is based on dependence. They believe that FOREX is easy and that they will achieve success quickly with little effort on their part. They possess a "bandwagon" mentality, believing that the preaching of some acclaimed FOREX guru or the purchase of a FOREX robot will provide them with instant wealth. They do not possess the ambition to investigate way of educating themselves about proper FOREX trading practices.

2. Beginners are normally attracted to FOREX by all the publicity promoting its enormous daily turnover. They fail to research the dramatic facts supporting this very high dollar figure. They see only a large treasure chest and pray that they can obtain a piece of the action. Consequently, their trading psychologies and abilities are way out of line and they usually quit trading FOREX sooner than later.

3. Novices do not understand that there is nothing inherently wrong with FOREX trading in and of itself. Generally, they are simply not prepared for the challenges ahead. They enter into FOREX trading with greedy aspirations, but the fear generated from successive losses eventually causes them to quit.

If you identify with any of the attributes of a novice, then you must strive to attain the correct education in order to join the ranks of the next group, the experts.

1. In contrast to novices, FOREX experts are in complete control of their trading and are fully focused on success. They always attempt to provide maximum protection for their equities by adhering strictly with their FOREX trading

strategies and exhibiting discipline and confidence at all times.

2. Experts research the work and experiences of others, but do not mimic. Instead, they possess the outright confidence to be able to select and competently integrate any new ideas into their own strategies, if appropriate.

3. Many experts start their FOREX careers by following a mentor or a well-constructed educational program. However, as their abilities develop, they become adept at producing their own FOREX theories and strategies by successfully sifting the workable items from the bad.

So, how can a novice become one of the elite 5 percent that are successful at trading FOREX? To achieve this task, many experts advise pursuing the following course of action:

1. Identify a number of credible educational sources that are easy to follow. You have achieved this step already by purchasing this book. Then get to work by studying a step-by-step guidance on how to construct a FOREX trading strategy.

2. Base your FOREX trading strategy on yourself and your lifestyle. Integrate these important features into your strategy from the outset.

3. Learn how to fully test your FOREX trading strategy by calculating its win-to-loss ratio and expectancy value. Then trade the FOREX strategy with a clear psychology that is not influenced by any emotional inputs.

The approach listed above will require investing a significant amount of time to master the essential concepts of FOREX. In addition, you should now be gaining a better appreciation of the subjects one needs to consider when deciding whether to become a FOREX trader or not. A novice must firmly believe that trading FOREX is a good career option and understand that a realistic approach to trading activities must be adopted from the outset.

Quite often, once FOREX beginners realize the vastness of their task, many become discouraged and give up sooner than later. Try to avoid this attitude. Indeed, it should not be forgotten that FOREX offers many desirable benefits that other types of trading do not. For example, there are large quantities of free educational information that is readily available. This is a huge advantage to beginners. In addition, here are some further reasons why FOREX trading is a very good option for those who have the perseverance to succeed at this very challenging but infinitely rewarding career:

1. FOREX generates sizeable price movements every trading day from which traders can target profits.

2. FOREX trades twenty-four hours a day, from 5:00 pm EST on Sunday to 4:00 pm EST on Friday, and enjoys significantly larger trade volumes during this time than any other market. A trader will never have any difficulties opening and closing FOREX positions because of the high levels of liquidity that are always present.

3. A FOREX broker is trained to provide clients with a high leverage facility that will enable a novice to open positions of significant financial worth with very small deposits. For ex- ample, with leverage of 100:1, a trader could buy or sell US$100,000 worth of currency with just a US$1,000 deposit.

4. In contrast, the stock markets post much smaller levels of liquidity [15] than FOREX, making developments such as breaking news much harder to trade accurately. Research also backs up the claim that as major financial institutions are informed about all developments on the stock markets well ahead of general traders, they can utilize this information to generate unexpected market movements.

Despite its many attractive attributes, one should never underestimate the complexities of FOREX. Many try to overcome the question of the market's complexity by purchasing a FOREX robot or employing a FOREX signal service.

There are many FOREX robots available that claim to have definite advantages over manual trading, such as trading without human emotions. However, your education will not stop if you try one of these solutions. In fact, most of these tools do not achieve anywhere near their claimed marketing results over the long haul. In fact, many are just outright scams.

It should be noted that FOREX is a very volatile market and predicting currency directions requires well-developed skills. This book advocates a good trading strategy comprised of a well-constructed set of rules that must be applied consistently with minimum emotional input.

Likewise, it is vital to acknowledge that all experts have a thorough educational grounding in FOREX. Indeed, nobody can simply leap into FOREX trading and expect success without a clue about what they are doing. Undisciplined and badly constructed trading activities will only generate stressful situations. The best way to combat the stress associated with trading FOREX is knowledge and experience.

This book will also clearly explains fundamental [16] and technical analysis, both of which aid in defining the best ways of utilizing a trading platform. Analyzing trading charts as a means of constructing an entry and exit plan for your FOREX trading strategy is also a very important skill to develop.

4.3 - Controlling Fear and Greed

All successful FOREX traders must learn how to control emotions such fear and greed. Indeed, both can have devastating impacts on a trader's chances of success.

For instance, introducing measures to minimize the impacts of fear is of the utmost importance, otherwise this emotion can paralyze one's ability to trade FOREX profitably. Novice traders often first encounter the negative effects of fear after suffering a series of consecutive losses. At this point, confidence levels began to fall as the trader's mind filled with an increasing dread of further failure. The best course of action is to develop solutions as quickly as possible that will combat the debilitating effects of this emotion.

Fear can dominate a novice's mind if risk levels per trade and potential losses as a result of price fluctuations have not been assessed. Fear can be combated if the impacts of a series of consecutive losses on your total account balance can be restricted and minimized. This objective is normally achieved by incorporating a well-tested money management strategy. Once achieved, fear can be controlled much more easily because the dread of sudden and serious losses of equity will be minimized.

Of course, mastering such skills does take time. Consequently, a novice who not willing to implement such changes is well advised not to become a FOREX trader. For instance, this book will aid in the design of a trading strategy that comprises a set of rules that can be used for consistent and confident trading. Such a tool will help in the suppression of fear because it will produce more gains than losses over the long haul.

Another method that will help restrict the impact of negative emotions is carefully maintaining a trading diary. Log all the details of trades, including feelings, for later analysis. Using such a technique will assist in boosting confidence and controlling emotions as it allows for the identification of both positive and negative trends. In this way, a trading strategy can be adjusted and improved over time. Never underestimate fear, as it is strong enough to make a novice trader divert from an otherwise successful trading strategy.

Following the above recommendations will help to separate you from the thousands of novices who fail quickly at FOREX trading. Dropping the cavalier "get rich quick" mentality for a more professional and business-like approach is certainly a step in the right direction. If you think that you can make such a transformation, then you should seriously think about becoming a FOREX trader and enjoying its many benefits.

For instance, one must accept the fact that the best decisions won't always be made, simply because of the complexities of FOREX trading. Preparation is key, as most novices quickly discover that many trading situations can generate undesirable emotions such as fear. Here are a couple of examples:

1. Learn to control the temptation to close open positions prematurely should price suddenly begin to move rapidly against them. This skill is not easy to master because novices often doubt their initial assessments and start worrying about sizeable losses. Counter such emotional responses by developing trust and faith in your newly acquired money management skills and trading strategy.

2. Similarly, don't panic should price initially proceed in the right direction, producing a profit in the process, but then begin to retract. Under such circumstances, don't interfere with the trade and prematurely close it unless your trading strategy advises you to do so. In many cases, price will resume its original direction, leaving you to observe lost profits in frustration. The following diagram provides a good example of a novice trader who panicked and sold at the wrong moment.

One cannot allow their emotions to ruin the hard work that went into producing a good trading strategy. What is the point of producing and testing a trading strategy if you constantly ignore its recommendations? Always strive to be mentally tough by developing total confidence and trust in the positive test results generated by your strategy. All FOREX traders experience losses, but a tested strategy will generate a greater number of wins than losses over the long haul.

Some traders attempt to remove their emotions by not monitoring their trades and simply walking away. They use a price target or stop loss, which is essentially an alarm system that alerts them when price reaches a designated condition. By doing so, they attempt to minimize all emotional influences from their trading and rely totally on the recommendations generated by their trading strategies.

Following the procedures described in this book will produce a well-tested trading strategy. After the strategy is created and tested, full confidence and trust must be placed in it, especially if price moves against any of your open positions.

With a well thought out strategy in place, a trader will not have to face a pending financial wipeout because each trade is simply another statistical event. Perhaps most importantly, a trader's equity will have maximum protection because of the development of a well-tested money management strategy, which will effectively minimize losses.

Greed is another dangerous emotion that can adversely influence FOREX trading. FOREX trading can be a very lucrative activity if one can develop methods to control greed. There are a number of different views about how this objective can be achieved:

1. Understand that greed causes traders to overtrade and, consequently, expose their equities to high levels of risk. Greedy traders set their sights on targets that are not readily

attainable and often go against the recommendations of the strategy that they may be using.

2. As with fear, greed can be controlled by designing a well-tested trading strategy that incorporates sound risk and money management concepts. This will help restrict the impact of gut instincts on a novice's trading activities.

One of the main causes of greed is the fact that traders are provided with a significant leverage facility by their FOREX brokers. As mentioned previously, this means that positions of considerable worth can be activated with just a small deposit. Unfortunately, many novices are not equipped to deal with these large sums of money and have a tendency to adopt a gung-ho approach by throwing caution to the wind and targeting one gigantic payout. However, please note that the protection of your own equity should be the number one priority.

Greed is one of the main reasons why so many novices fail at FOREX trading, losing their entire equities in the process. Here are a number of trading situations where greed is often experienced:

1. A trader opens a long position with a well defined stop loss and profit target. Shortly afterwards, price achieves the target value, realizing a good profit. At this point, the trader should always close the position and secure the profit.

However, a trader may not do this if greed sets in. This often happens when price advances further in the desired direction. The prospect of increased profit may make a novice trader maintain the position open. However, such a decision could be a mistake if it is based on greed and not derived as a recommendation from a tested trading strategy. Always remember that price can retract very quickly and destroy a profit in seconds. The following chart illustrates such a situation.

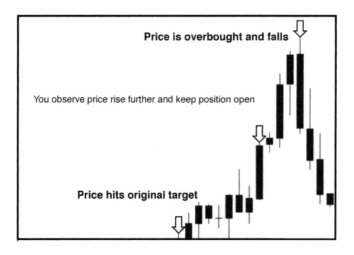

2. Currency pairs can generate price trends that may extend for some considerable time, from days to even months. These events can be excellent profit sources if handled correctly. However, the main difficulty when trading in such trends is that price can retract very quickly and without warning. Consequently, the novice trader must avoid greed by exiting trades at the moment indicated by the trading strategy.

Rational thinking must not be influenced by the greed generated from the sheer amounts of money traded on FOREX. Only those who have the commitment to counter and control their emotions should seriously consider becoming FOREX traders.

5

Developing Your FOREX Psychology

Developing Your FOREX Psychology

5.1 – How Novices Think

How well novices can advance their trading psychologies will be one of the main factors that will influence the size of the profits they will make from FOREX trading. In order to progress one's mindset from that of a beginner to that of an expert, a baseline is needed in order to track progress. The following list identifies the main characteristics of a novice's psychology and is therefore useful for generating a baseline.

1. Novices do not know how to implement the following FOREX maxim: "Let your winners run and cut your losses." Consequently, they usually register significant losses over the long haul.

2. Many novices become addicted to FOREX trading in the same way as other forms of gambling.

3. Beginners constantly feel that they do not control their trading. Instead, they simply pray, hope and wish for success.

4. Novices may even develop unfounded fears that FOREX is victimizing them, especially after they have endured a bout of consecutive losses. They begin to think that no matter what they do, FOREX will be there to force new losses.

5. Many beginners use borrowed money—or funds that they cannot afford to lose—to trade FOREX. This tends to

subject them to intense stress.

6. Even if beginners do win, they do not know how to deal with this event very well. They tend to become overconfident and consequently start overtrading, which in turn leads to serious losses.

7. Novices do not know how to calibrate their FOREX trading strategies properly.

8. Traders just starting out do not know how to master their emotions and generally allow hysteria and gut feelings to dominate their trading decisions.

9. Beginners become consumed by fears of failure after trading for some time.

10. Novices have normally not mastered the concepts of risk and money management. As such, their anxieties make them exit trades prematurely.

If any of the above actions or ways of thinking are familiar to you, they must be eliminated quickly. It is essential that one develops the mindset of a FOREX expert. Successful traders who are well versed in FOREX usually exhibit the traits discussed in the next section.

5.2 – Thinking Like an Expert

What are the benefits of developing a professional mindset? The following list answers this all-important question by identifying the main attributes of successful FOREX traders.

1. Experts maintain an open mind with regard to their trading activities as opposed to being dogmatic.

2. Professionals learn from the trading experiences of others but never mimic.

3. Successful FOREX traders know how to trade with the trend as a natural course of action.

4. They view winning and losing as central components of their trading strategies.

5. Experts enjoy FOREX trading because it does not cause them to feel any stressful emotions.

6. Veteran traders are in complete control of their trading and are under no illusions that they are being victimized.

7. Successful traders know that their skills must be continually upgraded through education.

8. They have a well-developed understanding of risk and money management concepts. As such, they never worry about their equities because they know they are well protected.

9. Experts possess an in-depth appreciation of leverage and always ensure that they never overtrade.

10. Successful traders know how to tweak and calibrate their trading strategies so that they can enjoy immediate benefits whenever they perform such tasks.

For many novices, attaining the mindset described in the above list is tantamount to achieving nirvana. However, it is important to note that thinking like an expert is certainly a reachable goal and one worth working toward. Expert FOREX traders reside in a mental space of profitability, tranquility and harmony.

5.3 – Benefits of an Advanced Trading Psychology

By now it should be clear that the proper mindset strongly influences one's ability to trade FOREX successfully. As such, being prepared by enhancing your mental approach is vital to coping with all the emotions and pressures associated with trading FOREX.

Novices can be better prepared for the battles ahead by simulating live trading as closely as possible from the outset. There is no point in using a demo account unless you trade the exact strategy you intend to use during real trading. The point of simulating live trading with a well thought out strategy is that it allows novices to feel the emotions and stress that will affect them psychologically when they go live.

One must develop the proper psychology during these early stages; it will pay off in the long run by fostering the kind of discipline, dedication and persistence that are necessary to guarantee success. The goal is to be able to study trading situations more objectively and hence improve trading decisions.

Although a given FOREX trading strategy may be sound, it will be useless unless it is combined with the right mindset. If one is unable to control the myriad emotions that often crop up during trading scenarios by working with discipline, then any strategy, regardless of its viability, is useless.

Many technological advances have been made during the last 50 years. However, it should be noted that throughout this period the high number of novices that fail at FOREX trading has remained essentially constant. The reason for this distressing statistic is that the majority of novices have not sufficiently developed their trading psychology. It's apparent that technology has continued to make our lives easier, but human nature has not changed very much over the last half century. Indeed, it's clear that FOREX does not beat traders—traders beat themselves.

In addition, this distressful failure rate will extend well into the future if novices do not take measures to remove their emotions their trading decisions. When live trading, knowing how to accept losses and not panic during a series of them. Losses are part of a trading sequence and are not a reason to abandon a tested trading strategy.

A trading strategy must be designed to help you keep losses small whilst allowing winners to run. Unlike demo trading, going live obviously subjects a trader's equity to risk. To counter the ensuing stress, strong discipline and confidence are required in order to adhere to your chosen strategy.

Using psychology when trading FOREX is not a new concept. Novices have just not realized the significance of the proper mental attitude. Understanding yourself is essential if you want to master FOREX trading. Novices that begin trading are essentially making both emotional and financial commitments. However, the impact of the former is often overlooked.

For example, if a trader has an ego, this will likely result in difficulties coping with losses. Indeed, it is very difficult to trade successfully when enduring such mental anguish. Although it is almost impossible to remove emotions completely from your trading, it is possible to make a concerted effort to control them.

5.4 – Focus On What Works

When people are first introduced to FOREX, they may be led to believe that its price movements can be predicted with relative ease. Obviously, traders would have excellent chances of obtaining serious profits if this fact were even partially true. Such oversimplifications entice many novices to commence trading FOREX without giving this career the consideration it deserves.

Does this statement have any merit, though? Certainly, FOREX does, in fact, produce strong price trends that are generated by such developments as improved risk appetite and safety flights. It is also true that research into the market psychology responsible for well-known FOREX patterns such as tops and bottoms would result in findings that would help in the fine-tuning of forecasting skills.

However, this task is far harder than most people think. In reality, FOREX generates price movements that do not obey simple or complex formulae. The confusion understandable, however, because FOREX does give the overall impression of some type of ordered chaos.

A serious study of FOREX trading will definitely verify that FOREX does create trends that exist for some extensive periods of time. As such, if you can devise techniques to detect trends, then you are certainly recommended to trade them. In fact, this type of trading is acknowledged to be one of the most profitable.

However, when novices do begin trading based on trends that they've identified, they often make the mistake of using trading charts that follow trends over very short time frames. Obviously, identifying trends over longer time frames is preferable due to the simple fact that one's chances for success go up as more information is learned about a trend.

Studying longer time frames generates superior and higher quality statistics that can better filter out the random noise produced by FOREX over the short term. Indeed, the problem of noise increases dramatically as time frames shrink.

A good piece of advice for those commencing FOREX trading is to utilize a daily time frame or higher. If this is done, the chances of identifying FOREX patterns will increase dramatically over using shorter time frames.

Although a currency pair may have been trending for some time, it may still be subject to vicious price oscillations generated by the minute or hour. In fact, a trend can be described as being comprised of a sequence of small price movements for the length of its existence. Beginners will find that they will continuously have problems if they favor shorter time frames because trading decisions will consistently be influenced by FOREX noise.

One of the main reasons that many novices opt for shorter time frames is that they think the increased level of action generated by FOREX noise will produce a larger number of profitable opportunities. However, FOREX statistics and historical data strongly indicate that this practice is seriously flawed and will only result in substantial losses.

The above advice is immediately applicable for standard FOREX trading techniques. Methodologies that target trading FOREX noise as their central concept are available. You may be attracted to methods such as scalping, but that is a different way of thinking.

5.5 – Getting to Grips with Reality

Many would-be traders start their FOREX careers by following the practice used by most novices, which is to first demo trade before advancing onto a live account. A recent survey that asked novices how long they planned to trade FOREX using their demo accounts before going live came up with some interesting results, as discussed below.

The results indicated that 10% of beginners intended to live trade immediately, about a third planned to use their demo accounts for up to two months, a second third preferred to demo trade for three to six months, about 20% intended to demo trade for one year and only about 5% claimed that they intended to demo trade for two or more years.

The above statistics confirm that about three quarters of all traders polled had intentions of trading their own money on the FOREX market within one to six months from startup. This result is of great interest because it correlates well with the staggering number of novices who fail at trading FOREX. It's also readily apparent that your chances of trading FOREX successfully are not good if you plan to go live after only one to six months of demo trading.

You may beat the odds and be successful, but be aware that historical records and statistics do not favor novices who demo trade for short periods of time. Indeed, six months may not be enough time to learn all the necessary information about FOREX trading. For instance, during this short period beginners have to learn, in particular, how to design and then fully test a FOREX trading strategy.

Consequently, those traders prepared to demo trade for one year or more certainly provide themselves with a more adequate time period to get a handle on the necessary education and training. As a result, these individuals have a much better chance of being able to manage their live accounts professionally.

However, even those that demo trade for a year or more still have to take in and assimilate vast amounts of information to ensure that they can produce steady trading profits. As such, even sufficient experience demo trading cannot guarantee success over the long haul, although it certainly improves the odds.

It is also important to note that one year of training may not be sufficient to develop an expert's grasp of the complex world of FOREX trading. Accordingly, novices may need to demo trade for a longer period of time before they are ready for live trading.

Devoting two years or more to demo trading may help novices bring their psychology into clear focus, thereby providing the optimum chances of success. If you fall into one of the first four groups identified by the study, you must now begin to adjust your mindset and prepare mentally to spend much more time becoming acquainted with complexities of FOREX before live trading.

Beginners should delay going live until they are fully prepared. Realize that FOREX is totally merciless and those who haven't developed the proper mindset usually lose significant amounts of money.

5.6 – Widening Your Horizons

Perseverance and determination are required to trade FOREX successfully because traders must contend with one of the most volatile markets in the world. FOREX cannot only generate very complex price patterns, but it can also alter course instantly and without warning. Indeed, hardly any other market reacts to world events in such a comprehensive way as FOREX does.

As mentioned earlier in this book, significant political events, such as a new government taking power, can generate substantial movements in a country's currency as it related to the currencies of other countries. This is because trading institutions can become unnerved by these types of events, resulting in a drop in confidence.

A currency's performance can be influenced by events— political coups, wars, new government policies and resource distribution, for instance—occurring within its host nation. Consequently, keeping abreast of international affairs is an integral part of any successful trader's fundamental analysis.

In addition, other influences that can strongly affect FOREX should be monitored. For example, many large investment institutions transfer money around the world in an attempt to at- tract the highest returns from investment vehicles. Should any negative international events occur that may trigger risk aversion, these corporations are also poised to seek safe havens for their capital. Such organizations include large banks, investment companies, governments and hedging funds.

These bodies have the power to generate severe price movements on their own because of the high dollar amounts they work with. Many traders attempt to deduce the intentions of these organizations by researching their shareholdings on the stock market. FOREX has a very strong correlation with the stock market even though it is a completely separate entity. For example, when the present lower-yielding currencies such as the YEN and USD rise, the Dow Jones Index [17] tends to fall.

FOREX can also be used as a gauge for evaluating the health of world trade and the global economy. Consequently, an appreciation of national interest rates, inflation levels and commodity prices serves traders well. Many have seen an increase in their FOREX returns as a result of studying such economic data.

Consistently making good quality decisions is the key to earning any worthwhile profits from FOREX trading. However, this task quite difficult if one's trading is solely based on monitoring all the considerations mentioned above. This is one of the main reasons why every trader needs a trading strategy.

To develop a trading strategy, you need a good understanding of technical analysis, which will then allow you to utilize technical indicators, detect major price structures and identify new quality trading opportunities. Every good FOREX trader is well-prepared because they have a clear grasp of the complexities of this market.

As in most professions, it's not worth it to take shortcuts in FOREX trading. Most novice traders find that FOREX robots or FOREX signal services eliminate some complications but introduce others. Instead, focusing on designing a good trading strategy is still likely the best avenue to pursue as it teaches novices to trade properly and independently.

6

Jumpstarting Your FOREX Career

Jumpstarting Your FOREX Career

6.1 – Rolling Up Your Sleeves

Sadly, there are no hidden secrets or shortcuts to help FOREX traders make quick profits. As a result, hard work is really the only way to devise profitable trading strategies.

When learning about FOREX, it is advisable to study other people's ideas and theories as many traders have already developed FOREX trading strategies that allow them to identify quality entry and exit points for their new positions. A little research into this topic will reveal that these strategies vary greatly in their ability to produce profits.

It should be reiterated that one of the best ways forward in gaining a solid understanding of FOREX is to design a customized trading strategy. The prime objective of designing a trading strategy is to detect as precisely as possible the entry and exit levels of bull and bear trends that extend for days, if not weeks.

As mentioned earlier, FOREX has a significant correlation with the stock market as both respond swiftly to any economic and political developments that occur worldwide. For instance, the Dow Jones Index rises when good news is generated, but drops in response to calamities. The concepts of fundamental analysis can aid in evaluating the influences of these global developments on FOREX.

When a novice begins to develop a FOREX trading strategy, the concepts of fundamental and technical analysis should be involved to some degree or other. Both methods are discussed fully in later chapters of this book. This chapter is designed to provide an introduction to the concepts involved in designing a trading strategy. Numerous diagrams will be utilized to help you easily gain a feel for this process.

6.2 – A simple FOREX Trading Strategy

Here is an example of the steps that should be followed when producing a simple strategy:

1. Locate renowned economists who are proficient at forecasting the impacts of fundamental events on FOREX.

2. Determine any synergies between their predictions and your own technical analysis of trading charts. For example, did the recent posting of an important economic event force any technical indicator to generate a crossover?

An analysis like the one discussed above can be performed by utilizing daily (or higher) trading charts. This is because, as mentioned earlier, statistical information from daily charts is of a much higher quality than that contained in charts that span shorter time frames. Daily charts also better facilitate the detection of major price formations, such as trends.

3. If your analysis does identify any correlations between your own findings and those of expert economists, you may have identified new quality entry or exit points for either bearish or bullish price trends.

4. If correlations between your findings and the work of economists have been found, activate a new trade by selecting a position size in accordance with your risk strategy. This subject will be discussed in depth in a later chapter.

5. Track the open position until your trading strategy informs you to close it. For example, you may exit the position when your technical indicator produces its next crossover.

The following chart shows a real trading situation that demonstrates the five steps above in action.

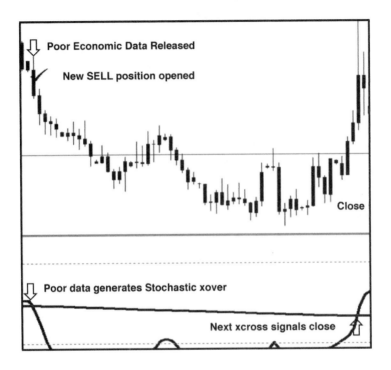

If a currency pair is exhibiting a bullish trend on its daily chart, it can be assumed that this tendency will continue into the future. In fact, one of the best methods of acquiring serious FOREX profits is to trade in the same direction as a trend. It should always be remembered that the earlier a trader can detect a trend, the better the opportunities of realizing larger profits.

6.3 – An Introduction to Technical Indicators

There is a large quantity of technical indicators that can be used to aid in the analysis of price movements. Popular indicators include the Simple Moving Average (SMA) [18], Exponential Moving Average (EMA) [19], Relative Strength Index (RSI) [20] and Stochastic Oscillator (SO) [21].

It should be noted that none of the above technical indicators can accurately predict FOREX movements all the time, especially if a trader does not have the necessary experience and skill to use them properly. A later chapter will discuss this topic in depth, but the sections below contains introductions to the popular technical indicators mentioned above.

6.4 – Simple Moving Average

This indicator displays values that are calculated by adding the closing prices of the last N period and then dividing the result by the number of N periods. The SMA is a lagging indicator that one may utilize to predict future price movements using past price data.

Many quickly discover that this indicator is more reliable and provides more accurate readings when it is used with an increased number of periods. However, when doing so, this indicator has the disadvantage of then responding more slowly to new price developments.

6.5 – Exponential Moving Average

After using the SMA for some time, many find that it is good for detecting FOREX trends but does not cope very well with price spikes. This is because its design stresses older price data as opposed to newer information.

To respond better to events such as spikes, traders necessarily much use a technical indicator that places greater emphasis on new price data. The EMA does just that and can therefore adapt much better to trading conditions that are prone to rapid price movements.

Traders generally appreciate the fact that no mathematical calculations are required when utilizing an indicator such as the EMA as charting software is capable of performing this task. The following diagram compares the SMA to the EMA.

Green line: SMA
Blue line : EMA

The EMA responds faster to price changes

6.6 – Relative Strength Index

One should not design a trading strategy that depends solely on the RSI. However, combining the power of the RSI together with other technical indicators and statistical tools could make for a trading strategy that can be very accurate at identifying new trading opportunities.

The RSI is able to track any currency pair, and the recommended settings for its parameters are 14, 70, and 30. Again, the best results will be obtained if the RSI is used in conjunction with daily charts or higher.

Traders are advised to open a new long position if the RSI drops below 30, creating a bottom and then bouncing back upward, as is illustrated in the next diagram. Similarly, accepted practice dictates that traders go short if the RSI rises above 70, tops and then retracts below 70. You must close your position when you detect the next opposite RSI crossover.

Open new BUY position

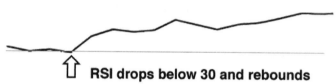

RSI drops below 30 and rebounds

The RSI performs well at detecting new trading opportunities whether it is incorporated in either simple or complex trading strategies. However, caution should be exercised because the RSI can often produce signals that are especially easy for inexperienced traders to misinterpret. Many experts advise confirming the RSI's by using other technical indicators in order to avoid any potential misreading.

Another problem with this particular technical indicator should be pointed out. Although the RSI may be posting a reading above 70 or below 30, it should be understood that price does not know this. As such, price could still continue to advance considerably in its current direction without the expected retraction.

Consequently, the currency pair in question could still surge by hundreds of PIPs as the RSI records only small changes (e.g., 70 to 74). Beginners and experienced traders alike must be acutely aware of this possibility. Indeed, if a new sell position is opened at RSI 70, for example, then a strong bull advance could stop out a trader's position very quickly.

6.7 – Stochastic Oscillator

SO is a technical indicator that is also very effective at detecting new entry and exit points if price is following a well-defined pattern. SO can be used to trade any currency pair and the recommended settings for its three main parameters are 14, 3, 3. Again, optimum results will be achieved if you deploy the SO on daily trading charts or those with higher time frames.

When the faster-moving stochastic climbs above the slower-moving one, open a new long position. Conversely, activate a new short position should the faster stochastic drop below the slower one. Close your position when you detect the next opposite crossover, as illustrated in the next diagram.

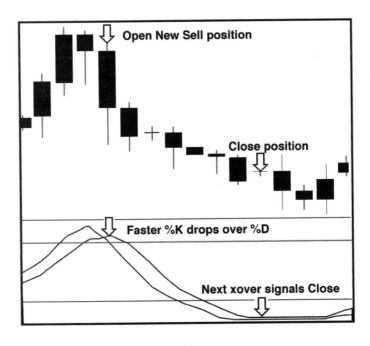

The SO is very easy to use and is a good tool for detecting new trading opportunities. However, the SO is a lagging indicator and can therefore generate signals that may be misread, especially by novices. Consequently, many find that the settings of the SO must be constantly tweaked in order to optimize its performance in relation to current market conditions. The SO can also generate the following problems:

1. Similar to the RSI, price can still advance rapidly in the opposite direction of a stochastic crossover. As the SO lags real-time, these events can be more difficult to deal with than those generated by the RSI.

2. As the time between the opening and closing of a position lengthens, the position may become very vulnerable to price movements such as spikes.

Under the circumstances discussed above, the SO may react too slowly and, as a result, may fail to alert you quickly enough. As a result, corrective measures must be taken promptly.

7

Selecting a Broker and New Challenges

Selecting a Broker and
New Challenges

7.1 – Types of FOREX Brokers

As previously mentioned, FOREX can be traded via a number of pricing levels, although the interbank market is reserved for large financial institutions such as central banks, corporations and hedging funds. With the advent of online trading, smaller traders can now gain access to FOREX using the trading platforms provided by retail FOREX brokers.

However, these new FOREX internet connections are not supelported by any stringent regulations in the same manner as the interbank market. Consequently, unscrupulous brokers can augment their returns by unethically interfering with their clients' trading positions. One of two types of brokers can be used to trade FOREX: Market makers provide their services by operating dealer desks, while other brokers employ ECNs.

Market makers are the more common of the two but do not provide direct access to FOREX. Instead they act as intermediaries to the interbank market. It's important to note that market makers perform this task by trading large units of currency on the interbank market and then supplying smaller units to the smaller traders. By implication this means that traders who employ the services of market makers may find themselves in direct competition with their broker when trading FOREX.

Needless to say, if such a situation were to arise, it would create a serious conflict of interest. Additionally, many traders mistakenly believe that their chosen market maker only achieves profits from their spreads. However, this is not always the case, because as market makers govern their own reserves of currency, they can control the price feed (bid/ask) available, which may place their clients at a disadvantage. The following problems may be encountered when dealing with a market maker:

1. Many traders find that the spreads they are offered may not be the most competitive because they are single-sourced.

2. Unscrupulous market makers may action unethical tactics, such as price spiking, in order to activate their clients' stop losses. Some market makers have also been known to increase spreads just as new trades are opened.

3. In general, traders dealing with market makers must always be on guard because these brokers gain increased profits if they utilize methods to expand the size of the spreads that they offer their clients.

Novices must also be aware of the distasteful act of re-quoting, which can occur at the moment a new position is opened. Unfortunately, a broker can detect their clients' trading intentions as soon as they activate a new trade. At that point, an unscrupulous broker can sometimes generate a new price for the trade that is inferior to the current quoted value.

Dynamic and volatile trading also breeds the right conditions for re-quoting because price can move so quickly. Traders may then experience delays in the execution of orders because their broker's computers just cannot keep pace with the real-time action.

Above all, beginners and seasoned veterans alike must gain assurance that their broker can consistently open positions at the quoted price displayed. If, when dealing with a market maker, you suffer from adverse effects such as re-quoting, then you would be advised to seek the services of another broker.

Of course, this isn't to say that all market makers are unethical. It must be kept in mind that there are good and bad brokers of this type. The best ones are on a mission to develop long-term relationships with their clients, and their demeanors communicate this. Conversely, if you're uncomfortable when speaking to a broker, listen to your gut feeling and shop around. The last thing any trader wants is to be taken advantage of.

The best way forward is to take your time in undertaking a thorough review of the services of each market maker of interest. This objective can be achieved by reading professional reviews and using demo accounts, if provided.

In contrast, ECNs can provide traders with direct access to FOREX while competitive price quotes from multiple banking sources. This type of broker differs from market makers in the following ways:

1. Although ECNs can provide real-time quotes from a series of large banks, many traders find that these quotes are not as stable as those offered by a market maker.

2. ECNs use multi-sourcing to supply clients with competitive spreads and prices. As ECN brokers do not directly compete with their clients, they do not need to manipulate trade results in order to produce increased profits.

In recent years, the popularity of some ECN brokers has surged because they have supported the MetaTrader 4 trading platform. Many novices find this feature of interest, especially if they plan to either buy or build a FOREX expert advisor or robot.

7.2 – Evaluating Brokers' Services

When selecting a FOREX broker, one must thoroughly examine its trading platform by using a demo account before even considering going live. By doing so, traders will get a good feel for the service they can expect once a real account is opened.

ECNs obtain profits by introducing buyers and sellers and charging a commission for their services. Their fee is usually generated in the form of a spread, which is the difference between the selling and buying prices of a currency pair.

No trader should underestimate the impact of spreads on FOREX returns. This is because every time a trade is opened, a trader must gain the spread in order to just break even. For example, if the difference between the ask and bid prices of the currency pair is 4 PIPs, then a trader would need to gain these four pips before they start to record a profit. The broker's commission for this trade is the four-PIP spread.

Spreads' sizes are recorded in PIPs and even the slightest increase in value can drastically influence a trader's profits. It is therefore important to seek brokers who constantly offer the lowest spreads possible. In addition, novices should trade the major currency pairs because they have much smaller spreads than more exotic currencies.

FOREX brokers are usually associated with large banks or lending institutions because they require substantial amounts of money in order to be able to provide leverage facilities for their clients. In addition, the better FOREX brokers are always regulated by the Commodity Futures Trading Commission (CFTC) and registered with the Futures Commission Merchant (FCM).

FOREX brokers can provide a variety of trading platforms comprising many different features, including technical analysis tools, technical and fundamental commentaries, real-time charts, real-time news, support and economic calendars. Most brokers allow potential clients to open demo accounts so they may experiment with the brokers' trading stations for free.

One of a broker's most important services is leverage, which is represented by a ratio that expresses the total capital available to a trader's deposit. Leverage is essentially the amount of money a broker is prepared to lend to a client in order to support trading activities.

For instance, if a broker is prepared to provide a leverage of 100:1 then this means that the client will have US$100 to invest for every US$1 they deposit. Consequently, the trader would be able to open a position worth US$100,000 with a deposit of only US$1,000.

Consequently, traders with limited funds will require a broker offering the highest levels of leverage. Otherwise, any reputable broker will suffice. Two types of accounts are usually available: a mini account and a standard account. A mini account will allow trades of US$1 per PIP as a minimum, whereas a trader would risk US$10 per PIP with a standard account.

It should be noted that there is another type of account sometimes available called a micro account. However, few brokers will actually allow traders to open one. A micro account allows trades of just ten cents a PIP. The ideal route when beginning to trade FOREX would be to progress from a demo account to a micro, and then onto a mini before opening a standard account. Risk levels can be readily controlled by progressing in this manner.

Upon opening a FOREX account, traders are required to sign a margin agreement verifying that they understand that they will be trading with borrowed money. This also means that the broker has the right to interfere with the account should trading activities go out of control. If such conditions do arise, then the broker will invoke a margin call, resulting in all open positions being automatically closed. Avoiding margin calls should be a top priority as such calls can result in significant losses for the trader. Such circumstances usually occur as a consequence of overtrading. Guidelines on how to prevent such circumstances from ever happening will be provided later in this book.

After enrolment is complete, the account must be funded before trading is possible. Prior to this stage, it's important to verify that the broker will provide good technical support. At the very minimum, a trader should have access to twenty-four hour telephone and email support.

It's a good idea to contact the help lines of a number of brokers before making a decision, asking questions about various service features. Assess the quality and speed of their responses and determine the relative quality of their services.

Many people trade with their own personal computers. In this case, it's important that a potential broker provides access to FOREX via the internet. The quality of all real-time FOREX quotes should also be a concern when choosing a broker. If a broker's real-time quotes were displayed on the FOREX 30 minutes prior to appearing, then obviously a better broker should be found. Needless to say, it's important that traders have access to the most recent price information in real time for all currency pairs. Never attempt to trade FOREX without this essential data.

It is also of utmost importance that traders are able to inspect their unused and used trading margins in real time in order to avoid overtrading and invoking margin calls. Ideally, traders should be able to see all the key parameters of their account in real time.

It is also necessary to obtain the quoted prices displayed when new positions are opened in order to safeguard against problems such as re-quotes. Consequently, any viable prospective broker should use a What You See Is What You Get (WYSIWYG) display.

It is also worthwhile to ensure that a broker provides two types of online access: one that operates using web-based software (hosted on the broker's website) and one that allows a trader to download the software to a personal computer.

One of the advantages of the web-based option is that it allows traders to access their FOREX accounts from any computer with an internet connection. On the other hand, downloadable software allows access to a broker's trading platform on a personal computer. Using downloadable software, traders will only be able to trade their FOREX accounts from their own computer.

One of the main advantages of the downloadable software is that it allows for faster access and execution than is possible when using the web-based option. Traders who prefer to use their own computers are well-advised to invest in the fastest internet connection they can afford (i.e., DSL or broadband). Dial-up is much too slow.

In addition, a broker should provide mini- and/or micro-lots. This will aid in the reduction of risk levels during the early stages of a novice's FOREX trading career. Any prospective broker should also enable clients to open positions using all the major currencies (i.e., USD, EUR, YEN, GBP, CHF, CAD, AUD, and NZD.

As mentioned previously, traders should look to brokers that can offer the smallest spreads. A broker's margin requirement should fall between 0.25 percent and 5 percent. It is also important that you research whether you will have to pay rollover charges. These are costs that are generated when open positions continue from one day's trading into the next. These fees are evaluated by calculating the difference between the interest rates of the base and counter currencies.

Finally, traders should ensure that they are able to access their accounts during the entire time that FOREX is open. It is important to ask if a broker allow trading continuously whilst FOREX is active, from Sunday 5:00 pm EST to Friday 4:00 pm EST.

7.3 – Coping with FOREX Volatility

Once a FOREX broker has been selected, an account has been opened and a trading platform has been downloaded, a trader will then have to contend with all types of trading conditions. One of the most challenging conditions a beginner can face is one that is generated during volatile times. This section will provide some guidelines about how to best cope under such circumstances.

When FOREX is stable, opening a four-lot position with a profit target of fifty PIPs may be an acceptable strategy if this action is in accordance with your risk management strategy. However, when FOREX is generating high volatility, it can produce oscillations that can exceed hundreds of PIPS per day. Consequently, a new strategy must be defined or positions may be quickly and constantly stopped out. Under such circumstances, consider reducing the lot size of trades in order to minimize risk levels. The next diagram compares stable trading conditions to volatile trading conditions.

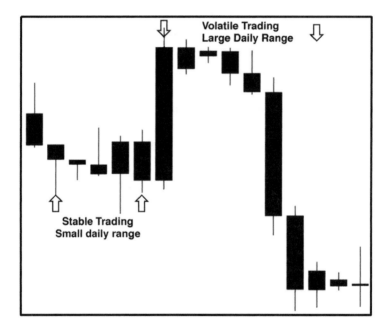

As previously stated, traders are always recommended to adhere to their FOREX trading strategies under all market conditions. This concept must be even more strictly enforced during volatile times. Indeed, in such conditions, the significance of imposing greater self-restraint should also be noted. If stress levels increase as volatility increases, following the main recommendations of your chosen FOREX trading strategy (i.e., risk management, stop-loss placement and contingency plans) without any hesitation becomes all the more important..

By following the trading strategy closely, a trader will be able to define and adjust risk levels should price generate more unpredictable movements. As mentioned, traders often suffer significant losses if they trade without strict discipline and self-control. Doing so could even place one's entire equity in jeopardy.

For example, a trader may not consider deploying tighter stops during volatile times because such actions would increase the chances of stop-outs. However, such a strategy could result in a better profit-to-loss ratio under these conditions. For instance, imagine a trader opens a long EUR/USD trade. If price action is volatile, you're a possible response would be to reduce the planned 100-PIP stop loss to a 50-PIP one.

By doing so, the new position would still be provided with a good degree of protection. However, it should be noted that a volatile price action is just as capable of stopping out a 100-PIP stop loss as it is a 50-PIP one should the market proceed against the position. In this case, the stop-loss reduction would successfully minimize risk exposure if a negative event were to happen.

Additionally, price spikes can occur even during stable trading times. As such, traders must always be on their guard to defend their equities against unexpected price spikes. For instance, some FOREX traders are large corporations or governments that possess very large budgets. Without any prior warning to traders, these institutions can produce considerable price movements or spikes on their own simply due to the immense size of their transactions. Always be aware of such activity and calculate your risk-to-reward (RR) ratio [22] accordingly.

7.4 – Using Demo Accounts Properly

FOREX experts always emphatically advise trading FOREX for some considerable time before risking money by going live. This can be accomplished by opening a demo account with a FOREX broker. Access will then be granted to the broker's trading platform, which should contain an extensive collection of free demo facilities and tools.

Novices who open demo accounts will also have the ability to evaluate and compare the trading platforms of all prospective FOREX brokers at no cost. FOREX brokers are more than happy to allow traders to do this because this provides them with the opportunity to present and advertise their services and tools with the overall aim of persuading possible clients to open a live account with them.

Although this concept sounds great and is definitely is a good step to take, there are substantial differences between utilizing a demo account and trading live. For example, demo trading does not generate the same emotional and psychological effects as live trading because no money is at risk. As such, many adopt a more cavalier approach to demo trading. In contrast, live trading can generate some extremely nerve-racking situations if significant, and real, financial losses are sustained.

When demo trading, such demoralizing events, which can badly influence confidence, are avoided. For instance, traders will not have to combat the increasing fear that develops when price suddenly starts moving against open positions. Worries about losing one's entire equity are not present because equity can always be replaced.

Consequently, a gung-ho approach to demo trading can lead to the development of potentially poor trading habits, such as trying to keep positions open indefinitely. It should go without saying that in a real trading scenario, such practices would not be a very good idea as one's equity remains exposed to high levels of risk.

FOREX experts also advise that beginners learn how to control their emotions when going live. However, this skill is difficult to master when demo trading. A trader's top priority when live trading should be to provide the maximum equity protection. This task can generate uncomfortable emotions that can have adverse effects on the quality of trading decisions. For instance, a series of consequent losses, which of course results in shrinking equity, can have serious influences on morale and confidence.

These problems can be combated by trying to ensure that demo trading conditions simulate those of live trading as closely as possible. For example, using a dummy balance of US$50,000 when demo trading could distort a trader's performance if this amount does not match the dollar figure they plan to use when going live. Instead, traders should always choose a sum that is more indicative of the size of equity that they will be able to provide when trading live.

7.5 – Preparing for the Challenges Ahead

Beginners should never feel deceived by thinking that FOREX is relatively simple to master. This is an easy trap to fall into because at face value, it appears that all a trader has to do is decide whether price will rise in value or drop. When traders forecast correctly, they make profits—when they don't, they lose. However, it should be clear at this point that determining whether prices will rise of fall is a task of some significant complexity.

A huge variety of people are involved in trading FOREX, from small individual traders up to large financial institutions and governments. It is important to note that no single institution on is capable of dominating a market the size of FOREX. In a very real sense, then, small traders are on the same level as all other traders, including the big ones. As a result, FOREX can be a very exciting market in which to trade.

At the same time, traders have to master a number of very complex skills in order to trade FOREX successfully. Fortunately, there are measures that novices may take to stack the odds in their favor and achieve real progress. This is certainly possible, but only if all initial preconceptions are washed away. FOREX is not an easy subject to master, and considerable amounts of time must be invested in order to gain any headway in this very competitive market.

Novices that have just commenced FOREX trading or have experienced problems trading it successfully must halt any and all live trading activities immediately. It is advised to revert back to demo trading and commence redesigning and improving a trading strategy. Beginners should use the demo trading tools the broker provides to simulate live trading conditions as accurately as possible, as described above.

Traders who feel that they need to demo trade for only a couple of months are seriously underestimating FOREX. It's a fact that professionals such as lawyers and doctors take many years to master their craft. Likewise, novices should not expect to absorb all the intricacies of FOREX in a short amount of time.

Instead, would-be traders should advance their skills by using demo accounts and targeting realistic objectives. A good rule of thumb is that traders are ready to go live when they constantly record profits that have not been manipulated in any way. An excellent understanding of such FOREX concepts as time frames, fundamental events, trading strategies, leverage and technical indicators is required to live trade successfully.

For example, it's always a good idea to avoid overtrading by utilizing good risk management. Study each FOREX topic fully until gaining complete mastery over it. Restricting one's risk level per position will provide the maximum protection against losses. Furthermore, as mentioned previously, beginners must not underestimate the benefits of education and should seek to consult quality sources on the topic of FOREX whenever necessary.

Novices should not even contemplate live trading until they are fully confident and competent at making consistent profits while demo trading. Always remember that FOREX is a volatile market that can crush traders' positions unless they are fully prepared.

7.6 – Next Steps after Opening a FOREX Account

As this chapter has already described, traders can gain access to FOREX through a broker regardless of the amount of equity they have at their disposal. This dynamic opportunity has been available to everyone since the introduction of the Internet.

Consequently, those entertaining a career in FOREX trading now have an excellent chance of achieving extra income by trading from home.

However, novices need to consider whether they feel they will be able to learn how to trade FOREX well enough to register worthwhile profits consistently. It should be noted that everyone is capable of profiting from FOREX trading provided they educate themselves properly and gain enough experience. Indeed, FOREX experts the world over agree that learning to trade FOREX successfully is an art that requires effort and time to master.

There are a number of places where beginners can locate quality sources to acquire a FOREX education without being scammed. The Internet is certainly a possibility, but be aware that about 50% of all books and training courses on the Internet are of poor quality. Some information contained or sold on the internet may even be considered fraudulent.

Be wary of material that suggests that FOREX trading can be mastered easily by learning a few simple techniques. Most of these products have been written by individuals or companies that have failed at FOREX. Seek only educational material that has been produced by FOREX experts who can actually demonstrate real success at FOREX trading.

As can be expected, quality choices will result in quality teaching material that provides information about all major FOREX subjects, including the effective use of equity. Many sources also offer good recommendations about developing and fully testing a FOREX trading strategies while keeping risk levels under tight control. Every novice must master the art of distinguishing good educational material from bad. Without this vital skill, losses of both money and time will likely result.

Many high quality FOREX books have been written by acknowledged experts. Consulting these sources is an excellent place to begin because as the initial financial outlay of most novices is quite modest. Many would-be traders find that starting with these types of books also offers the advantage of being able to learn about FOREX their own pace.

Before purchasing any products, attempt to confirm the quality, integrity and effectiveness of the material by reading the opinions of other traders. Search for reviews and opinions on these products by visiting the many online forums and message boards available on the Internet.

7.7 – Assessing Trading Platforms

Different traders have different needs, and it's important that brokers are able to satisfy those needs. One of the major services to consider is the quality of a broker's trading platform. This essential element allows traders to access FOREX so that they can open and close trades. Consequently, a prospective FOREX broker must be capable of providing a trading platform. If, for some reason, a broker does not offer a trading platform, other options should be explored.

The design of trading platforms involves complex technology and mathematics. As such, beginners should find a platform that is relatively easy to learn and that won't interfere with trading activities. Novices generally require a tool that will allow them to commence trading quickly without the necessity of studying large manuals. A novice also needs to confirm that their chosen platform will be able to support their trading strategy and that the platform's construction is not too rigid to hinder defined objectives.

Beginners already have a steep learning curve to contend with before mastering FOREX trading. Learning how to properly use a complicated trading platform while still learning the basics about the market itself is not recommended. From the outset, it should be clear that a platform will not obstruct your trading abilities and skills, but rather enhance them.

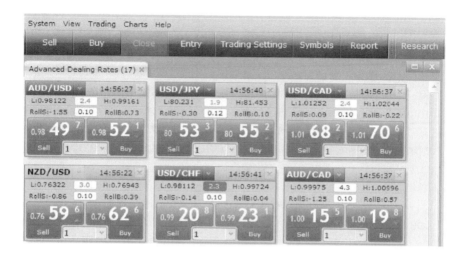

The above diagram displays a good toolbar from a trading platform that provides many useful facilities and is easy to read and navigate. In addition, a broker should supply clients with a good quality charting facility. The following diagram shows such a package, which again provides an easy-to-use toolbar. Ideally, a trader should be able to open and close trading positions directly from the charts provided by the broker.

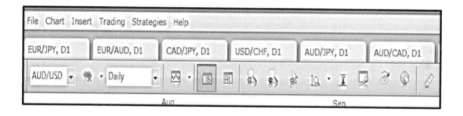

Even beginners must be able to gain swift and unimpeded access to FOREX. Consequently, all the buttons, tools and switches of a platform should be self-explanatory, just as their intended functions should be easy to learn. Contending with a complex and hard to use FOREX trading platform will only compound problems for a novice trader.

Trading platforms often feature designs that can be quite involved because they comprise complex algorithms that at-tempt to simulate the FOREX environment. A good platform should be able to generate immediate responses to any command, despite these complexities.

For example, a command that activates a new position at a specific entry level should result in a trade that is open immediately at the chosen price. If this is not the case and the new entry price is some distance from the desired price, another broker should be investigated.

As FOREX can produce rapid price movements, you're a trading platform must not hinder trading activities to any degree. Indeed, traders using overly complex trading platforms will have significant problems determining how to generate consistent profits from FOREX. Consequently, a FOREX broker must be able to supply clients with service of the highest quality. As explained, this includes providing an excellent trading platform.

7.8 – Using Small Steps of Increasing Risk

Thorough surveys into the methods used by FOREX traders have led to the discovery that there are a number of main reasons why so many novices lose their initial account balances quickly after startup. Understanding how to avoid these problems will result in significant strides toward becoming a member of the decidedly small band of FOREX elite.

For example, novices must prevent themselves from being distracted by unproven tools and ideas. Instead, attention should be focused on developing a clear path forward that includes gaining access to high quality educational resources.

Additionally, traders should never overestimate their FOREX skills and knowledge. Although someone may have a good level of proficiency in some FOREX subjects, this does not automatically equate to success at FOREX trading. As previously mentioned, the subject is very complex and capable of generating equally complicated price movements.

It is always a good idea to listen to what this market is really trying to do as opposed to guessing. Keep trading simple by not utilizing FOREX trading strategies that are too involved. Traders who attempt to do so often discover that they lose sight of the overall price action. Of course, this could easily generate adverse effects on trading results.

In contrast, the best course of action is to develop a simple trading strategy and then improve its performance by tweaking one of its key operational parameters at a time. This allows for the evaluation of any improvement by determining the expectancy value of the strategy after each test.

While improving your trading strategy, skill levels should also be improved by using steps of small incremental risk. Begin with a demo account, then a micro account (risking 10 cents per PIP), next a mini account (risking US$1 per PIP) and finally move to a standard account that risks US$10 per PIP. This process will no doubt take some time, but will provide the optimum chances of mastering FOREX.

Trading FOREX successfully requires complete commitment and taking responsibility for any and all trading actions. In particular, this means coming to terms with and understanding the implications of any losses suffered. Constantly searching for shortcuts by either jumping on the bandwagon of some self-proclaimed guru or utilizing purchasing robots will do nothing to enhance and perfect your own FOREX knowledge and experience.

Traders should never depend fully on any single fundamental or technical technique. Implementing the good ideas of others into a trading strategy to create something that is stronger than the sum of its parts is a very valuable skill. Dismiss all the marketing campaigns that promise a quick path to riches by trading FOREX.

Learning how to practice patience from the outset will pay dividends later on, as this is a trait required of all successful traders. The first step in developing patience is to persevere with the trading strategy that you develop. Ensure that it is traded and tested thoroughly before moving onto a new, untested tool.

8

Risk and Money Management

Risk and Money Management

8.1 – An Overview

Once a trading strategy has been devised, acquiring a very good understanding of the concepts of risk and money management is vital to success. No matter how well a given trading strategy may perform, it can still be improved greatly by merging it with a good money management strategy.

A risk and money management strategy can be used as a statistical tool to help calculate you how much should be risked per trade. For example, risking too large a proportion of one's total equity per trade may result in missing the full benefits of a trading strategy's positive performance if positions are continuously registered losses.

After designing a good money management strategy, it should be used in combination with the following important FOREX concept: Do not risk too much of your balance at any one time. Traders who follow this advice greatly improve their chances of advancing their FOREX skills and knowledge in small steps of incremental risk while ensuring maximum equity protection.

Many experts recommend that novices adopt a simple money management strategy that advises against ever risking more than a pre-determined and fixed amount of their total account balance on any single FOREX trade. In particular, 2 percent is the maximum recommended.

Risk per trade can be kept within this specification by correctly calculating the stop loss and position size of each trade entered.

The stop loss specifies the number of PIPs a trader is prepared to risk per trade, while the position size represents the size of the trade expressed in lots.

8.2 - Preventing Margin Calls

One of the reasons why risk and money management is so important is that these concepts can be used to prevent margin calls. Indeed, margin calls can be one of a trader's biggest problems when setting out on a FOREX career. Taking serious measures to eliminate margin calls must therefore be a top priority.

A margin call will be activated if a client's trading activities become so out of control that they begin to expose the broker's money to serious risk. A margin call is generated if the trader's useable margin plummets to zero, meaning that the trader does not have sufficient funds left to support any trades that may be open. Should such an event occur, all open positions will be closed immediately. In addition, if any trades were posting negative values at the time of closure, the unfortunate trader's balance will be reduced by their combined loss. In fact, receiving margin calls is one of the fastest ways to completely obliterate one's entire equity.

After experiencing the demoralizing influences associated with margin calls, motivation and confidence will have to be restored before trading can commence. This may not be an easy process as margin calls can produce long-term negative psychological effects.

When most people start trading, they quickly discover that margin trading has some inherent advantages because it allows for the use of FOREX leverage, which permits traders to open new trades of considerable worth with just a small deposit. For example, if a broker provides leverage of 100 to 1, then a new US$100,000 position could be opened with a deposit of only US$1,000.

Although this concept sounds very impressive, it should be

understood that there are serious problems associated with the use of leverage should price move against open positions. If a novice overtrades and price advances extensively against one or more long positions, the broker will issue a margin call that will automatically close all open trades, resulting in the possibility of serious losses.

The best way to prevent margin calls is to design and utilize a sound and well-tested risk and money management strategy that will prevent overtrading and consequently avoid high levels of risk. Novices should also teach themselves to control dangerous emotions such as greed, as such feelings do not influence the quality of trading decisions. Unfortunately, FOREX's high daily turnover can easily seduce beginners into making decisions based on emotions as they gamble unrealistic sums of money.

The FOREX market is a very dynamic environment that is capable of generating periods of high volatility. Consequently, these high levels of volatility combined with leverage can produce emotionally charged situations that can result in overtrading if caution is not practiced at all times.

In fact, margin calls and the misuse of leverage are two of the prime reasons why so many beginners fail at FOREX, losing their entire initial equities in the process. Risk levels per trade must be well-restricted under these conditions if one is to avoid margin calls. This problem can be neutralized by utilizing a well-constructed risk and money management strategy.

Fundamentally, traders must restrict the percentage of their equities that they will risk per position. How can one determine what is a good risk level? To answer this question, consider the following example.

There is a serious difference between risking 2 percent of total equity and 10 percent of it. For instance, risking just 2 percent of total equity would result in a loss of about 17 percent should a trader be unfortunate enough to endure ten consecutive losses. Under the same conditions, but risking 10 percent of total equity, the trader would experience losses of about 66 percent.

After studying the above example, it should be clear that using a lower level of risk per trade will certainly help minimize margin calls and optimize equity protection. This is the very reason why so many experts stress the importance of risking a maximum of 2 percent of total equity per trade.

8.3 – The Mechanics of Money Management

One of any trader's top priorities should be understand the essential nature of money management to a successful FOREX trading strategy. Unfortunately, most novices fail to completely understand this important concept and a large portion of them fail as a consequence. One of the best ways to succeed at FOREX trading is to design or acquire a trading strategy that contains mechanisms to cope with the following aspects of trading: money, mind and method.

More specifically, a management plan based on selected elements of technical analysis will help to control and protect your equity (money), while developing the right psychology (mind) will foster the kind of patience and discipline that is required to carry out the trading strategy (method) successfully.

Novices who do not devise a money management strategy have a tendency to focus only on method because they tend to base their decisions on trading charts. As a consequence, they completely overlook the money and mind aspects. This means that their final products are usually flawed and result in failure most of the time.

A FOREX trader's top priority should be equity protection, because without it, the FOREX game can't be played. However, human nature tends to prompt people to concentrate on profits as opposed to focusing first on potential losses. In addition, most novices suffer from a psychological tendency to believe all their trades will be winners. Consequently, they completely ignore what should happen if problems arise.

As FOREX is so complex, it should be accepted that losses are practically inevitable. Successful traders are those who perfect the art of controlling their losses by managing them properly. Again, this is why a money management strategy that will minimize risks while maximizing profit potential is so important.

Coming up with a good money management strategy is crucial to achieving FOREX success, especially because of the high leverage and volatility involved in the market. Always remember the following FOREX maxim: "Take care of your losses, and the profits will come by themselves."

FOREX trading is all about probabilities and traders only have full control of their equities until the moment they open a new trading position. From that moment onward, price rules the day. No one can know for sure whether their trade will achieve a profit or loss. However, a well-tested money management policy, gives traders the ability to determine the maximum loss they may suffer should price turn against their open positions.

A money management strategy should be based on two simple concepts: a well-determined RR ratio and correct position sizing. The latter parameter represents the amount of equity will risk per trade and is measured in lots.

A trading strategy should possess a minimum RR ratio of 1 to 2. If a higher RR ratio can be achieved, then this is preferable. The following example will illustrate the concepts involved in determining an RR ratio.

It should be acknowledged that losses are an unavoidable part of trading. As such, assume a strategy exhibits a win-to-loss ratio of 50 percent, which implies that five out of every ten positions are winners. To ensure constant profits, a trader would have to aim to record profits in accordance with the 2:1 RR ratio. Consequently if it has been determined that stop losses of 60 PIPs will be used, 120-PIP profits must be targeted.

If these conditions are realized, then the trader will suffer five losses of 60 PIPs each, but enjoy five wins of 120 PIPs each. As such, a total profit of 300 PIPs, despite enduring five losses, will be achieved.

8.4 - Recovering from Consecutive Losses

One of the most debilitating FOREX experiences that anyone—especially a novice trader—can suffer is coping with a series of substantial and consecutive losses. Many beginners actually achieve some success during their "honeymoon period" with FOREX. Unfortunately, the thrill of producing profits has the tendency to breed overconfidence and, as a result, the majority of these novices then suffer serious losses.

Once this demoralizing trend sets in, many traders begin to rack up a sequence of losses that they have great difficulty in correcting. The main reason that this occurs is because traders tend to become greedy after enjoying a positive run. They then start to overtrade by risking more than their equities can support. Traders in this position also have a tendency to treat their profits in a more cavalier way than they do their own funds.

It's a well-documented fact that many novices also try to combat losses by increasing the position sizes of each subsequent new trade. However, unless a trader has addressed and corrected the central reason for past failures, the only thing increasing position sizes will do is accelerate losses in larger amounts. This is a sure route to losing significant equity.

When one experiences this depressing sequence of events, it can be said that the most dangerous, and often hidden, foe is equity drawdown. Not only does this parameter generate a serious compounding factor, but it impacts on the amount of profits required in order to simply break even. The following table illustrates the dangers of account drawdowns by considering the impact of consecutive of 10-percent losses on an original equity of US$20,000.

It should be apparent from studying the above table that the

Account Balance	% Total Loss	% Profit Need to recoup original equity
$18,000	10%	11.1%
$16,200	19%	23.4%
$14,580	27%	37.1%
$13,122	34%	52.4%

impact of drawdowns is a compounding effect that can destroy an account very quickly due to the fact that profits need to increase exponentially following each new loss in order to simply break even. As the value of the trader's account plunges, recovery becomes much more difficult, if not impossible, if the same failing strategy is used.

To correct the situation, dramatic action is required. For instance, the trading strategy used should be discontinued immediately. Patience and a long sequence of consecutive small wins will be required to emerge out of a mess like this. Below are some methods that traders normally use to resolve this problem.

Many traders attempt to trade their way out of this difficult situation by opening new positions utilizing higher levels of risk. However, by doing so they are merely risking more on trading strategies that have already been proven to be flawed. This could be considered a form of gambling. As such, it is prone to disaster in the long term.

Another technique to overcome the drawdown problem is to inject new capital into the account. However, the wisdom of such an approach is questionable because the central problem— the inability to trade FOREX successfully over the long haul—has not been addressed. Consequently, this solution really just places funds at serious risk.

Most experts recommend that this problem be corrected

by going back to the drawing board and reassessing the failing trading strategy. In addition, any thoughts of swift profits should be thrown out the window in favor of a new approach that involves increasing the risk level per trade in small incremental steps. Focusing on developing skills and controlling losses is the best way to gradually recoup equity.

If injecting new funds to inject new funds in order to stave off margin calls is necessary, ensure that the amount is as minimal as possible. The main objective is to produce evidence of consistent profits, and the best way to do this is to take small, well-controlled steps. Any other approach is essentially giving FOREX the power to blow your equity out of the water.

In addition to the above, the development of a correct mindset is required to fend off intimidation at the sight of a falling account balance. Many novices do not emotionally handle such events well and have a tendency to adopt methods that will quickly eliminate the "evidence." One such solution is to inject large amounts of new funds into their accounts. Resist this temptation at all costs because it does not solve the central problem. Instead, adopt a policy that involves taking one small step at a time back to safety.

Upon mastering the art of achieving one small profit at a time, a trader's position can be recovered. More importantly, perhaps, is the fact that equity can be built using exactly the same strategy. Always focus on developing skills and resolving the central problem.

8.5 – Managing Your Profits

Many beginners spend a considerable amount of time studying how to enter new positions without considering a good strategy of how to exit them. Indeed, there is more to this skill than meets the eye because of the elements of human nature that are involved.

For instance, many become concerned if price has suddenly moved against a position. Under such circumstances, fear may make a trader exit the position prematurely before price continues in its original direction. Of course, frustration then sets in as the trader witnesses serious profits amassing that are now impossible to access.

Many traders can also attest to the fact that they've experienced greed at one time or another. Greed often encourages traders to cling to a position in the hope of increased profits, even after a well-tested trading strategy has issued clear exit signals.

To overcome the above problems, a trustworthy exit strategy with some scientific basis must be devised. The following section explains how to create such a strategy.

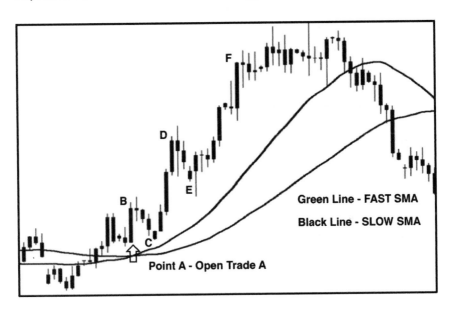

The above diagram illustrates the psychological problems that traders have to deal with when they do not have a well-prepared exit strategy. Imagine that a trader detects that the fast SMA rises above the slow SMA and subsequently opens a new position. Price proceeds to Point B, producing a good profit. However, instead of closing the position, the trader decides to keep it open in the hope of greater gains.

As can be expected, fears start to mount when the trader next observes price retracting to Point C. to the trader panics, closing the position at this point. A small profit may have been registered, but nowhere near that which could have been secured at Point B.

The trader's emotions rise once again as the price advances back in the original direction. As a result, a new position is opened towards Point D. However, before the trader can react, price again reverses back towards Point E, stopping out the new trade in the process. So far, this has already been quite an emotional roller coaster of a day!

Again, the price accelerates back in its original direction and the trader opens yet another new position between Points E and F. Unfortunately, price now undergoes a complete reversal, meaning that a loss is sustained on this position as well. After a lot of hard work, next to nothing has been achieved.

A better method of trading and securing your profits is required. One way of achieving this objective is through using support and resistances levels. In the next chart, resistance levels are defined at R1, R2 and R3. If selling, price will often rebound off resistance and support levels.

Imagine now that the trader goes long just after the SMA bullish crossover. Now, however, the trader closes the position after price touches R1, securing profits. The trader then waits for price to firmly reach R1 before opening a second bull position. If it does not, the trader is now protected from a serious price reversal.

A new trade is now opened about 20 PIPs above R1. If price now advances and hits R2 as it does in the above diagram, the trader again closes the position and once again makes a good profit.

Next, for the trader waits for the price to achieve a serious break of R2 before entering a third trade about 20 PIPs above R2. Once price reaches R3, the position is again closed and more profit is made. Additionally, if only 2 percent of total equity were risked per trade, the trader would have been fully protected throughout if price had fully retracted at any point.

The chances of success can be improved even more by always trading with the trend. For instance, one should only open buy positions when price is following a bullish trend. Conversely, only should only open sell positions when price is following a bearish trend. This can be done by utilizing two technical indicators, as is shown in the next diagram below.

A faster moving SMA and a slower moving SMA are used to achieve this purpose. A bullish trend can be detected when the faster SMA (represented by the green line) is above the slower one (represented by the black line). Conversely, a bearish trend can be detected when the faster SMA is below the slower SMA. Always remember that the trend is your friend, and trading with the trend will often produce profits.

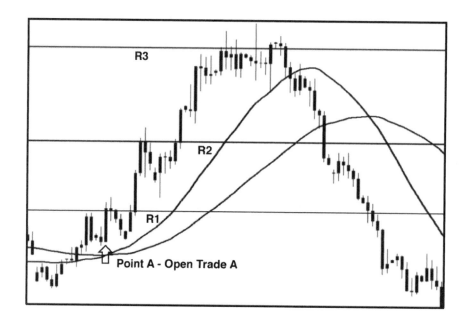

R3

R2

R1

Point A - Open Trade A

After studying the above examples, it should be clear that there are many advantages to using a well-constructed exit strategy. There is a vast amount of quality educational material available that discusses many other factors, such as different time frames and other technical indicators, that will help in the creation of an enhanced exit strategy.

8.6 – Different Styles of Money Management

There are two basic methods of money management that can be utilized to trade successfully. The first method will involve acquiring profits from a few large winning trades supported by small stop losses. The second involves targeting many small profits using very large stop losses so that the total of many small profits will exceeds that of a few large losses.

Which particular a trader chooses will depend greatly on personality. Experts have designed trading strategies that work well with both approaches. Regardless of the method chosen, persevering and not giving up at the first sign of difficulty is very important. Also note that the cost of each transaction is identical whether it is big or small. This is because FOREX is a spread-based industry.

For instance, when deciding to trade the EUR/USD currency pair, many discover that its spread is often quoted as 3 PIPs. Consequently, this spread size will be constant whether trading a large or small position. However, as a trader's cost equals the spread size times the PIP value times the position size, then it will increase with the size of the trade.

For example, let's say a trader is using a standard account and risking US$10 per PIP. If a one-lot trade is opened, a commission value of 3 (spread size) times US$10 times 1 (lot) will be charged. In this case, the commission value is US$30. Consequently, opening a twenty-lot position will result in a commission charge of US$600.

Consequently, traders can select various styles of money management because FOREX supports uniform pricing and variable transaction costs are therefore not a concern. When developing a money management strategy, design it about four types of stops described below.

8.6.1 - Chart Stop

Good stop losses can be determined by studying the trading charts of any currency pair of interest coupled with technical analysis. The following chart displays a bullish stochastic crossover. Under such circumstances, you're a stop should be positioned about 20 to 50 PIPs below the most recent low.

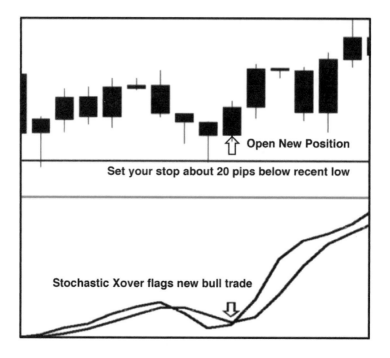

Open New Position

Set your stop about 20 pips below recent low

Stochastic Xover flags new bull trade

8.6.2 - Equity Stop

The equity stop is the simplest type of stop loss. Using the equity stop will reduce risk per trade to a preselected proportion of total equity.

As already stated, most experts recommend limiting risk per trade to a maximum of 2 percent of total equity. For instance, a trader with a balance of US$10,000 should aim to risk a maximum of US$200 per trade. If the trader is using a mini account, each PIP will represent US$1. Consequently, the stop could be placed about 200 PIPs away from the opening value while still complying with a well thought out risk and money management strategy.

However, using this stop method means a trader basing your trading strategy on your own internal risk strategy. This is contrary to defining a stop loss that is logically deduced by identifying key technical features concerning price action.

8.6.3 - Volatility Stop

The volatility stop is a more sophisticated stop that, as the name suggests, is based on volatility as opposed to price. This stop will give a position additional room during volatile times when price may fluctuate widely. This will help prevent a trade from being stopped-out as the result of increased noise levels. In addition, should volatility decrease, then this stop loss will also do so by compressing its risk elements.

Bollinger bands [28], which will be explained fully in a later chapter, may be used to help monitor volatility. In fact, this technical indicator is one of the most popular methods because it price variance by utilizing standard deviation. When volatility is high, the distance between the lower and upper Bollinger bands increases and may be quite large, as is illustrated in the next diagram.

In the case below, the volatility stop was placed below the black line, which represents a distance that equals the distance between the lower and middle Bollinger bands. As the size of the stop loss may be quite large under volatile trading conditions, a smaller position size may well have to be utilized in order to accommodate the strategy of restricting risk to a maximum of 2 percent per trade.

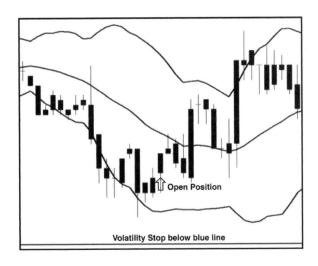

Open Position

Volatility Stop below blue line

The next diagram shows trading conditions during more stable times, when volatility levels are much lower. Notice that the distance between the upper and lower Bollinger bands has shrunk considerably when compared to the previous diagram. you're the volatility stop can now be positioned at a distance below the opening value that is equal to the distance between the lower and middle Bollinger bands.

If the stop is positioned as described above, the size of the stop loss in PIPs will be much smaller because volatility levels have dropped. Consequently, a bigger position size in lots may be selected while still complying with the 2 percent risk strategy.

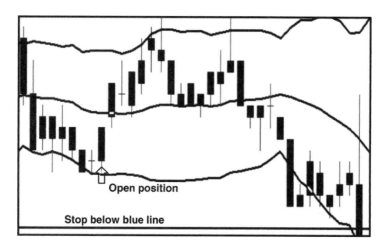

8.6.4 - Margin Stop

The margin stop is perhaps the strangest type of stop loss. Nonetheless, it can be very effective if used properly and with skill. To understand how it works, a few important features of FOREX must first be explained.

For instance, FOREX can be traded 24 hours a day, from Sunday at 5:00 pm EST to Friday at 4:00 pm EST. During this time, a FOREX broker can automatically close down a client's open positions by issuing margin calls should a trader's activities go out of control. Consequently, there is no real danger of ending up with a negative account balance.

To use the margin stop, total equity must be divided into ten equal parts. Next, a trader's FOREX account must be funded with one tenth of total equity. The rest should be left in a bank account.

When the next position is opened, its position size should be selected so that a margin call will be made should price activate the margin stop. Selecting a healthy-sized stop-loss will give the position ample room to breathe.

Should a margin call close the position, the procedure is the repeating using the next one tenth of equity. This is a strange way to trade FOREX, but some experts have achieved good success using it. As always, persevering with one's chosen trading selection is the key to generating the optimum chances for success.

8.7 - Business Risks

FOREX is similar to all other types of business in that it involves substantial risks and the serious possibility of fiscal loss. A business risk can be a situation, issue or factor that can have a negative effect on a company's trading performance.

There is a variety of external and internal factors that can contribute to risks in a FOREX setting. Developing good management policies should be a priority in order to always keep business risks under control.

Recognize that FOREX is viewed to possess above-average risk levels that exceed those of most other businesses. This is because FOREX can generate significantly high levels of trading volatility coupled with the availability of high leverage facilities. Consequently, traders are in constant danger of suffering serious losses should price turn against their live trades.

No one can ever completely eliminate risk from FOREX trading, despite all the strategies and tools that are available. As mentioned previously, this is why risk and money management policies must be used to the end of equity protection. In particular, novices and experts alike should never trade with borrowed money or capital that they cannot afford to lose.

The activity of trading FOREX carries with it a variety of risks. For example, despite the efforts of many, FOREX is a market that remains swamped with scams. Indeed, an army of sellers are constantly promoting courses, books and automatic solutions to a myriad of problems that can only be solved through hard work and experience.

Anyone considering trading FOREX should always perform comprehensive checks on any prospective FOREX broker. For instance, research must confirm that a broker is, at the very least, a component of a much larger financial organization, registered on-shore and a member of recognized and established bodies such as the National Futures Association, the CFTC or the Better Business Bureau.

It is also important to ensure that a prospective broker possesses a world-class proprietary price feed that can supply very competitive spreads. After selecting and enrolling with a FOREX broker, a trader's account must be funded before trading can commence. Once done, the trader will then be provided with an extensive leverage that could exceed 1:100. Leverage will enable positions of substantial value to be opened with just a small deposit.

However, leverage facilities bring with them a serious business risk if price turns against a trader's positions. Consequently, always remember that because FOREX can generate the most complex of price formations within very short periods of time, appropriate measures must be taken to minimize risk.

It is also important to take into consideration any changes in the interest rates of countries when trading their currencies. Specifically, monitor any such developments from the time a position is opened to the time it is closed. Indeed, changes in interest rates can influence profits.

In addition, note that traders are at the mercy of their

FOREX brokers when it comes to receiving fair value spreads because brokers are the ones who determine execution prices. The importance of choosing a trustworthy broker cannot be understated because FOREX has no central exchange exhibiting regulatory controls.

It is also necessary to evaluate the risks that may result should your FOREX trading platform falter in part or in whole. For instance, how would your equity cope if you were unable to cancel your open positions or activate new trades at vital times? If connecting to FOREX is reliant upon the Internet, consider the effects of margin calls or even fraud should trading be impossible at critical times?

Traders must also contend with other types of risks as well. For instance, a trader's credit may be at risk should any of the other bodies involved in FOREX transactions fail to service their debt at closure. For example if one of the parties went into bankruptcy, this could generate a significant amount of risk for a trader. Experts and novices alike also have to contend with risks related to trading currencies from certain countries as governments sometimes decide to restrict currency flows.

Always attempt to minimize risk exposure by acquiring a good understanding of the main elements of technical and fundamental analysis. All the concepts, facilities and tools that make up these two subjects should be used to restrict losses when trading FOREX.

As mentioned, this objective can be achieved by designing a well-tested risk and money management strategy. Such a policy should include well-defined stop losses for all new positions in order to protect equity should price turn.

All traders should treat FOREX trading as a business in order to restrict risk. Many experts agree that the best way to accomplish this goal is to compose a business plan that will assist in defining both risks and targets. The business plan should concisely list objectives, why these objectives are achievable and how the objectives can be achieved.

Important decisions should then be based on the concepts stated in the business plan. A trader should decide on the best format and content for a business plan by considering the targeted audience while at the same time ensuring the plan comprehensively covers all planned FOREX trading activities.

Subjects that may be included are finance, educational requirements, intellectual property management, human resource management and technical considerations, among others. Indeed, a better understanding of FOREX and your own intentions can be gained by creating a business plan.

A business plan will also aid in the development of a more professional and business-like approach to trading. Obviously, this will help better protect equity. Traders generally find that producing a business plan helps them significantly by minimizing the chances of failure when trading FOREX.

9

Fundamental Analysis

Fundamental Analysis

9.1 – Defining Fundamental Analysis

As this book has already advised, a trading strategy should be created in order to improve prospects in the FOREX market. Many traders utilize fundamental analysis to help them perform this task. This type of price analysis helps to predict future currency movements through the study of political, environmental and economic developments that may influence their basic supply and demand.

In other words, fundamental analysis strategies facilitate the determination of how political and economic events will influence FOREX. Consequently, novices should learn how to identify and then evaluate the release of important news information in order to assess the possible impact on currency pairs. Items of interest are political developments, new economic policies, economic growth forecasts, inflation and changes in interest rates.

Monitor the relevant statements and figures provided in speeches made by prominent economists and politicians. In particular, focus on any important announcements concerning the US economy and politics because they will generate the biggest influences on FOREX. For instance, speeches made by the Chairman of the USA Federal Reserve Bank and the US Secretary of Treasury can cause dramatic price movements.

Many considering a career in FOREX trading may already be aware that the currency of a country appreciates in value against other national currencies in response to good news while falling in relation to other currencies in the case of adverse developments.

Consequently, a wide range of information pertaining to the health of a country's economy should be studied if a trader is to predict the movements of that country's currency in relation to the currencies of others. For instance, it is helpful to analyze government policies and future plans, as well as track important economic indicators such as international trade, CPI, durable goods orders, gross domestic product (GDP), PPI, PMI and industrial production, among others.

After this data has been examined, a model needs to be developed that will help determine the effects on the present and future values of the applicable currency. Traders who can achieve these objectives will be in a strong position to determine if a currency will rise or fall against others on the FOREX market.

Consequently, utilizing fundamental analysis requires a focus on evaluating how all important global political and economic developments will influence the movements of currency pairs. One must also gain an intimate feel and understanding of fundamental analysis in order to use it well. Many experts advise combining fundamental analysis with technical analysis to some degree or other in order to help create a well-rounded trading strategy.

9.2 – Trading Economic Data Releases

The release of important national economic data is highly anticipated by the markets and can produce significant price movements. Prime examples of these types of events that are regarded by traders as of the utmost importance are US non-farm payroll announcements, national interest rate changes, the release of US unemployment figures and changes in US trade balance dynamics.

Such postings can generate rapid price surges or spikes, and this is especially the case if the data released pertains to the US economy. Substantially large price movements are produced if the new posted values surprise the markets by being higher than the anticipated figures produced by economic experts. In contrast, should the figures be similar, the price movements produced tend to be less notable.

Consequently, accurately forecasting the price movements generated by fundamental data releases certainly improves a trader's ability to profit from trading FOREX. However, this task is not easy to accomplish consistently without the necessary skill and knowledge. This fact holds especially true for novices.

One of the reasons why movements are difficult to predict is that a large number of participants contribute to produce price movements on FOREX, each with their own agenda and some with extensive budgets. This is especially true when highly important or classified economic data is released. This section will explain why this is so and provide insights upon which solutions can be based.

To commence this process, getting a grasp on a good definition of exactly what this information contains is important. Basically, portraying trader should look for news items that convey the latest insights into a country's economic health, either directly or indirectly. News releases are normally classified into three types: economic, political and financial.

Financial and economic news postings have the largest influence on FOREX and are eagerly awaited by all serious investors because of the impacts they can produce on the price movements of currency pairs. As already mentioned, this is especially true if the released values differ to any serious degree from experts' predictions. Consequently, all major data is kept under very tight control and in utmost secrecy until the exact moment of release because of the ensuing impacts they may have on the markets.

Whether a trader decides to use fundamental analysis or not, a top priority must be to know when all major data releases are imminent. This can be ensured by gaining access to the global economic calendar, which lists the exact times and dates of all data releases. A good FOREX broker will readily supply this information using a format similar to that shown in the following diagram

Tues Nov 2	03:30 LIVE	AUD Reserve Bank of Australia Rate Decision (Nov)	High	4.75%	4.50%	4.50%
	08:55	EUR German Purchasing Manager Index Manufacturing (OCT F)	Medium	56.6	56.1	56.1
	09:00	EUR Euro-Zone Purchasing Manager Index Manufacturing (OCT F)	Medium	54.6	54.1	54.1
	09:30	GBP Purchasing Manager Index Construction (OCT)	Medium	51.6	53.0	53.8
	22:30	AUD AIG Performance of Service Index (OCT)	Medium	50.7		45.6
Wed Nov 3	08:15	CHF Retail Sales (Real) (YoY) (SEP)	Medium	3.8%		0.1%
	08:30	GBP Purchasing Manager Index Services (OCT)	Medium	53.6	52.6	52.6
	12:15	USD ADP Employment Change (OCT)	Medium	43K	20K	-2K
	14:00	USD Factory Orders (SEP)	Medium	2.1%	1.5%	0.0%
	14:00	USD ISM Non-Manufacturing Composite (OCT)	High	54.3	53.5	53.2
	18:15 LIVE	USD Federal Open Market Committee Rate Decision (NOV)	High		0.25%	0.25%
	21:45	NZD Employment Change (QoQ) (3Q)	Medium		0.5%	-0.3%
	21:45	NZD Unemployment Rate (3Q)	Medium		6.7%	6.8%
	22:45	NZD Employment Change (YoY) (3Q)	Medium		1.2%	-0.1%
Thu Nov 4	00:30	AUD Retail Sales s.a (MoM) (SEP)	Medium		0.5%	
	08:00	EUR German Purchasing Manager Index Services (OCT F)	Medium			
	08:00	EUR Euro-Zone Purchasing Manager Index Composite (OCT F)	Medium			

The best facilities will allow traders to use filters to tune in to those events of utmost interest. A good idea is to focus attention on all events of high importance, regardless of the country. Of course, note both the high and medium postings produced from the US because most of them can significantly affect FOREX.

Traders serious about performing fundamental analysis well will also make a point of locating a source of real-time commentary that can provide analysis of the implications of all new economic and political postings. The following diagram illustrates an example.

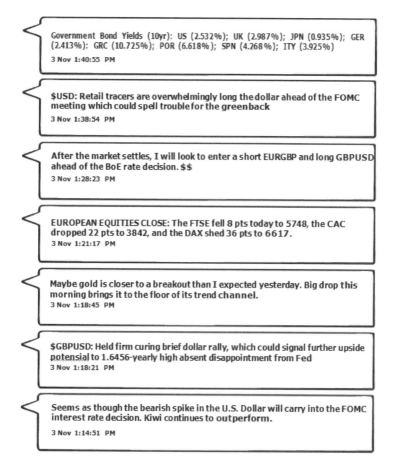

Government Bond Yields (10yr): US (2.532%); UK (2.987%); JPN (0.935%); GER (2.413%): GRC (10.725%); POR (6.618%); SPN (4.268%); ITY (3.925%)
3 Nov 1:40:55 PM

$USD: Retail tracers are overwhelmingly long the dollar ahead of the FOMC meeting which could spell trouble for the greenback
3 Nov 1:38:54 PM

After the market settles, I will look to enter a short EURGBP and long GBPUSD ahead of the BoE rate decision. $$
3 Nov 1:28:23 PM

EUROPEAN EQUITIES CLOSE: The FTSE fell 8 pts today to 5748, the CAC dropped 22 pts to 3842, and the DAX shed 36 pts to 6617.
3 Nov 1:21:17 PM

Maybe gold is closer to a breakout than I expected yesterday. Big drop this morning brings it to the floor of its trend channel.
3 Nov 1:18:45 PM

$GBPUSD: Held firm curing brief dollar rally, which could signal further upside potensial to 1.6456-yearly high absent disappointment from Fed
3 Nov 1:18:21 PM

Seems as though the bearish spike in the U.S. Dollar will carry into the FOMC interest rate decision. Kiwi continues to outperform.
3 Nov 1:14:51 PM

Political events can also seriously impact FOREX. For example, G-7 and OPEC meetings, national disasters and government elections should be developments of which traders are aware. Of course, it's easier to deal with events that are forecasted and scheduled well in advance. It is, however, a slightly more complicated matter dealing with unexpected developments such as terrorist attacks. These types of events can generate sudden and volatile market conditions.

Be aware that traders often have a habit of responding immediately to the headlines of a data release. Consequently, their instant reaction is capable enough to force price to surge in a particular direction.

However, this action is normally quickly reversed after the same traders have taken their time to analyze the details of the posting in depth. In addition, some data releases are comprised of multiple items. Consequently, complications arise when some components of a news release closely match their anticipated figures while others do not.

When this happens, traders can become confused and choose one solution initially, only to reverse their decision completely sometime later. As a result, it is important to guard against false price directions that are selected just after a release because they could be retracted dramatically within a short period of time once traders have a clearer understanding of the release's implications.

It should now be apparent why many traders, especially novices, experience difficulties coping with the vast permutations, complexities and nuances related to price movements. Indeed, in order to protect their equities from dramatic price movement, many traders do not get involved with economic and political events.

In particular, novices have a tendency to seriously overestimate their skills in trading fundamental events successfully because they mistakenly think that they possess the ability to accurately forecast outcomes. Unfortunately, this is not the case because their trading psychology contains the following flaws:

1. They tend to focus on potential profits only and ignore down- side risks.

2. Novices think that all the new trades will be winners and make them rich.

3. Beginners fail to realize that they will achieve greater success if they aim for more realistic targets.

4. As novices possess such high profit expectations, they often become quickly demoralized after experiencing a

sequence of consecutive losses.

As mentioned, economic data releases can sometimes generate significant price movements for currency pairs, although the reason why this happens is not always obvious. However, because these changes can persist for some time, traders are advised not to jump to the conclusion that the market is hot and open new positions on this basis alone. This is not a very good idea and can generate serious losses, especially if current market conditions are not fully understood. Sadly, this is a trap into which many novices fall.

Most traders, especially novices, should not attempt to trade fundamental data releases because of the significant risks involved. Always remember that the only factor that is 100 percent predictable about FOREX is that it is totally unpredictable. The posting of fundamental data events certainly supports this statement because the price movements that they can produce are completely random.

Does the above assertion make trading fundamental data releases a complete waste of time? No. If a trader is experienced and educated, the rewards can be well above average. The following is a strategy that many experts have perfected to produce consistent profits through trading fundamental data releases.

1. Wait until about 5 minutes before the release of the data and then activate both sell and buy entry positions about 25 PIPs on either side of the present quoted value of price for the currency pair that will be most affected by the posting. Also, enable price alerts 20 PIPs beyond these entry points.

2. Entry points may require tweaking in order to maintain their 25-PIP distance because price tends to fluctuate prior to a release.

3. If one of your positions is opened after the release, move

the stop to a 1-PIP profit position once its associated alert has been activated. Next, cancel the other trade.

4. These actions have resulted in a small profit. Lock in further profit if price advances in the chosen direction.

Traders should be cautious, however, because although risks may be minimized by utilizing such a strategy, this type of trading is still difficult because data releases can generate price movements very quickly. Consequently, this type of strategy requires good money management skills that include restricting risk per trade to a maximum of 2 percent of total equity.

This policy must be enforced when trading fundamental data releases because their unpredictability can produce so much uncertainty. Traders should also record the details of all trades related to fundamental data releases into a trading diary.

A diary is useful for reviewing results and determining the expectancy value of a trading strategy. Another useful piece of advice is to gain confidence in trading fundamental data events by back-testing your trading strategy against historical data. The realization that powerful data releases can influence the direction of price for a considerable time leads many traders to develop a strategy that will allow them to successfully trade the applicable currency pair during less turbulent times.

Many experts also advise either securing profits by either closing open positions or locking them in just before a major economic data release is scheduled to occur.

9.3 – Volatility and Economic Data Events

Those who intend to trade major news releases require a FOREX broker who can supply fixed spreads and fast command execution. This is because these events can produce very volatile conditions that can sometimes generate large price spikes. Unfortunately, most traders do not have sufficiently fast price feeds that are powerful enough to handle the market conditions that exist after major economic data releases.

The FOREX market can become very active around the times that important economic data is scheduled for posting because many participants are attempting to define their positions by transmitting an extremely large volume of orders within a short time period. Consequently, smaller traders' orders could be lost in the mayhem if the FOREX connections utilized are not of the highest speed.

A slower connection results in commands that may not be actioned until sometime after price has surged through a trader's planned opening level. In addition, there may simply be no sufficient liquidity existing on FOREX to satisfy the large number of commands that are being requested. Indeed, these difficulties occur often when volatility is high because of the impending release of important economic data.

Many traders try to identify new opportunities by utilizing one or more technical indicators as integral parts of their trading strategy. However, all of these tools experience problems coping with the high levels of volatility that FOREX can produce because they were not initially designed with this purpose in mind. Always remember this fact when attempting to trade major news events.

A trader should not regard technical indicators as the final answer to all the problems that are present during this type of trading. Technical indicators have been designed to perform best during more stable times when the statistics that they depend on are far more reliable. Traders who rely too heavily on technical indicators realize sooner or later that they do not fare so well when important economic data is posted.

If a trader does rely on technical indicators, is it possible to modify and update them so they can better handle volatility? Without superb mathematics skills, the simple answer is no. The best advice is to integrate technical indicators into a well-rounded trading strategy. The key parameters of the strategy can be tweaked until its performance is optimized. Furthermore, a trading strategy's performance should be reevaluated after each test by recalculating the strategy's new expectancy value.

In summary, it is paramount that traders gain an appreciation of the difficulties that can arise during the volatile times produced by the release of important economic data. Always remember that FOREX is capable of generating the very complex price formations that can demolish ill-planned trades in a matter of moments.

9.4 – More Trading Ideas for News Releases

After an economic news release, one may trade FOREX based on the idea that after the market has finally decided the real impacts of a major news item, it finally chooses its preferred price direction. Those who use this technique gain the benefit of not having to contend directly with all the emotional stress that can arise before, during and after major news releases. To activate this strategy, wait until about 20 minutes after the posting and then open a position in the current direction of the currency pair that has been most influenced by the release.

However, be cautioned against using this trading method just after the release of very important news items such as US non-farm payroll announcements. This is because such events can produce extensive volatility that could take an extended period of time to settle down.

Many people attempt to trade news releases by trading the initial direction of a currency pair after a retracement. Should the released number significantly differ from its anticipated value, then this result usually generates a price spike in one direction or the other, depending on the result released. In many instances, the initial price surge is often quickly followed by a complete reversal due to profit taking.

Consequently, traders are advised to wait for confirmation that this retracement is fully complete before opening a new position in the original direction of the initial surge. By doing so, the trade should enjoy an increased RR ratio as a result. As there is no exact method available to identify the precise end of the reversal, many experts recommend using either of the following two strategies:

1. Search for signals that indicate that the reversal is beginning to consolidate.

2. Wait for the currency pair to recommence moving in its original direction by a predetermined amount (e.g., wait until it has recovered half of the retracement).

In the above scenario, a very good spot to locate a stop loss is just below the bottom point of the retracement. A trading strategy can also be designed based on the concept that before the release of important news items, currency pairs have a tendency to start range trading within a tight consolidation pattern. The following diagram illustrates a particular event wherein traders were waiting for a US Federal decision to provide them with the confidence to either buy or sell the EUR/USD pair.

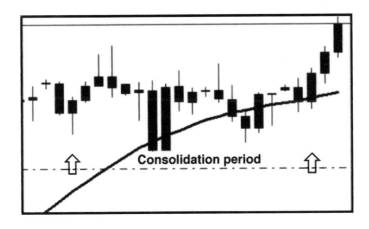

The above trading phenomenon is caused by traders waiting for the anticipated news release to provide them with the information to determine in which direction they should push the price. Consequently, if a trader can confirm that a currency pair is range trading by detecting a price ceiling (resistance) and a floor (support), some worthwhile profits may be earned before the news event occurs. However, be aware that price has a tendency to drift in one direction or the other just before an event.

For example, if traders expect that an US news item will be positive, then the EUR/USD may begin to display a sequence of lower lows and lower highs. Although fakeouts can sometimes happen in these circumstances, they seldom develop into full breakouts before the news events occur.

Using such a strategy is risky because economic data postings are notorious for producing wild price fluctuations. As mentioned, this is because many FOREX traders often fail to fully understand the significance of a release at the outset. Traders' opinions tend to change after releases have been examined more thoroughly.

Again, it is important to utilize a well-tested money management strategy to counter the above problem. However, do not be deterred by because the difficulties inherent in trading news releases. This strategy can be a very profitable if performed correctly.

There are three major techniques commonly associated with this type of trading: pre-, post- and spike trading. As the last one is deemed to be complex, concentrate on the ideas expressed in this section to gain proficiency in pre- and post-trading.

10

Technical Analysis

Technical Analysis

10.1 – Introducing Technical Analysis

Technical analysis in predicting future price movements through a study of the historical data records of currency pairs of interest. Doing so brings the full picture of the trading history of a currency pair into clearer focus. Indeed, even those traders that prefer fundamental analysis will still utilize technical analysis as a verification method.

It should be noted that technical analysis depends on a few theoretical ideas. For instance, technical analysis is centered on price movements and related data, and does not involve the opinions or attitudes of FOREX traders in any way whatsoever.

This type of analysis is also based on the fact that history has a strong tendency to repeat itself, producing price patterns that are predictable to a certain degree. A trader's main objective when using technical analysis is to identify new quality trading opportunities by detecting these predictable patterns.

Many experts agree that currency pairs move in trends, meaning that their oscillations are not chaotic and display some sort of order. For instance, many experienced traders that detect price moving in a certain direction usually believe that it will continue to do so for some time unless a major event occurs to prevent this action.

If technical analysis is incorporated into a trading strategy, it will facilitate trading in a more scientific and business-like manner. Although this type of analysis is by no means flawless, it can assist traders in setting better objectives and making quality trading decisions.

A number of different types of charts can help when performing technical analysis. Some of the more popular charts are described below.

1. A chart can be set to display the very popular candlestick pattern [24], with each candlestick displaying the closing, opening, high and low prices for the period of time being studying. The distance between the opening of the red bear candle and its high is termed the wick, while the distance between the red bear candle's closing and low is named the tail.

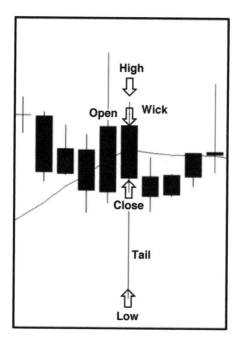

Candlesticks are extremely useful technical indicators, as is evidences by the fact that they have been used in trading for hundreds of years. During this time, many patterns comprised of candlesticks have been identified. The diagram below illustrates some of these patterns.

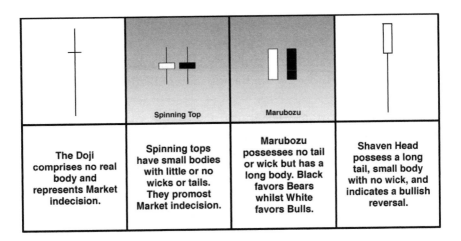

| The Doji comprises no real body and represents Market indecision. | Spinning tops have small bodies with little or no wicks or tails. They promost Market indecision. | Marubozu possesses no tail or wick but has a long body. Black favors Bears whilst White favors Bulls. | Shaven Head possess a long tail, small body with no wick, and indicates a bullish reversal. |

Traders tend to achieve more success with candlesticks if they are utilized in conjunction with trading charts that use the daily time frame or higher.

2. Alternately, a bar chart [25] may be used to determine trends. Bar charts also show the closing price, low price, opening price and high price of each time, as illustrated in the following diagram.

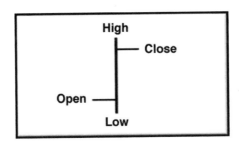

10.2 – Confirmation Using Candlesticks

This book has already introduced a number of techniques to safeguard equity while increasing profit potential. However, once a new possible entry point for a trade has been detected, it is good practice to seek additional confirmation before taking further action.

Many experts recommend that one good way to undertake this task is to examine the Japanese candlestick patterns on the daily trading charts of any currency pair of interest. You have already been introduced to the basics of candlesticks.

Ideally, one must seek confirmation that supports given new entry theory in order to determine that the new position has a high chance of success. During this procedure, the analysis should be as objective as possible.

For instance, do not enter a new position just be- cause you think it "feels right," especially if major technical events and items are indicating the opposite. Traders using such a system will only experience significant failure over the long haul.

A much better approach is to examine trading charts carefully and objectively for possible entry points. After determining what appears to be a viable entry point, it is important to seek confirmation by studying the candlestick patterns on the trading charts of the applicable currency pair.

In addition, if none of your trading strategies are displaying any evidence of new trading opportunities, study trading charts for positive candlestick patterns. If one is located, start researching into the reasons why these patterns have been formed (i.e., fundamental or technical factors). It is also recommended to reexamine chosen trading strategies in order to identify any backup evidence that suggests these candlestick patterns are advance warnings of potential new trading opportunities.

There are many books on the subject of candlestick formation. This section distills the pertinent information into one readily accessible source. Candlestick patterns can be used to detect and confirm key FOREX formations, many of which are discussed in this book (e.g., retracements, reversals, breakouts and fakeouts).

For instance, great use can be made of candlesticks to help determine reversals and retracements, as well as distinguish between the two. Indeed, there are a great number of candlestick patterns, and a few more popular ones are discussed below.

10.2.1 - Morning Star

This pattern is created by a three-day candlestick formation that identifies a strong bullish reversal. The first day is normally a long bearish candlestick, the second drops slightly lower and the third is a bullish candlestick that closes above the midpoint of the first candle, as is shown in the next diagram.

10.2.2 - Dark Cloud Cover

This is a bearish reversal pattern comprised of a large bear candle that casts a shadow over a preceding bullish trend. To create this pattern, the final-day candle in the sequence must open at a high and then close below the midpoint of the body of the preceding day, as is illustrated in the next diagram.

10.2.3 - Hanging Man

This pattern has a small body and occurs at the end of a bull run. Traders do not consider the color of the body to be of high importance and tend to be more interested in the fact that the long, lower tail is at least twice the length of the body and that there is

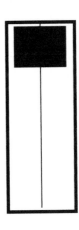

little or no upper wick. An example of a hanging man pattern can be found in the next diagram. This pattern is considered to be a bearish sign, indicating that there has been a strong attempt to sell long positions that was only reversed towards the end of the candlestick's time period.

10.2.4 - Shooting Star

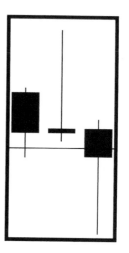

This pattern is created when the opening, low and closing prices of a candlestick are very close to each other. The shooting star's other main feature is that it has a long wick and is usually twice the size of the body. See the central candlestick in next diagram for an example. This is a bearish sign as it indicates that a bull movement was strongly rejected by the market.

10.2.5 - Doji

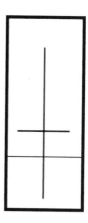

This pattern is formed when it opens and closes at its average price in the middle of its structure. The Doji possesses both a tail and wick that can be quite long and almost equal in length, as is shown in the next diagram. On its own, the Doji pattern is neither a bearish nor a bullish indicator. As such, it is generally analyzed as part of a three-candlestick pattern.

10.2.6 - Hammer

This pattern is created at the end of a strong downtrend and as such signifies a bullish reversal. The hammer has a very small body that is formed toward the end of the current day's trading. There is no upper wick to speak of, but a significant lower tail exists that is at least twice the size of the body. Essentially, a hammer pattern shows that the market price has bounced higher after hitting a possible support level. The next diagram show a hammer pattern.

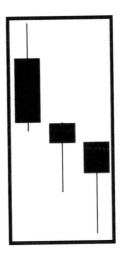

10.2.7 - Inverted Hammer

This pattern is a bullish reversal sign that occurs at the end of a strong downtrend. The day candle has an open and a close that are very close to each other, with a non-existent tail and a wick that is at least twice the size of the body. See the central candlestick in next diagram for an example of an inverted hammer pattern.

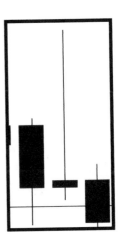

Candlestick patterns that have either a long wick or tail with hardly any body are the most useful (e.g., hanging man, hammer, morning star and inverted hammer). Traders are advised to try to detect these patterns on daily trading charts and higher.

These candlestick patterns can be used in a number of ways. For instance, if you have been unable to activate any new trades using your trading strategies, then searching for one of the patterns listed above is a viable alternative. Imagine that a hammer is identified on a daily chart. The reasons behind its formation should be investigated by studying all the support fundamentals, up-and-coming news and technical aspects. From this study, it may be possible to determine if a full-blown reversal is developing or just a relief dip.

Sometimes, if a trader has other reasons for entering a trade, candlestick patterns on the trading chart of the applicable currency pair should still be consulted for additional confirmation. For instance, suppose a trader were planning to enter a bullish trade after studying the daily charts but then notices that a morning star candlestick was forming. Under these conditions, it may be wise to reconsider and wait for further developments before proceeding.

Using this candlestick method can help in the detection of new trades, confirm open positions and warn against entering trades that will eventually transform into losses. However, it must be noted that candlestick patterns have limited use when key economic news releases are scheduled.

The effectiveness of introducing candlestick confirmation into trading strategies can be confirmed in the following way. First, calculate the expectancy value of the trading strategy and then repeat the process, this time including an extra step by introducing candlestick confirmation.

10.3 – Identifying Bottoms and Tops

When trading FOREX, imagine that price is moving in a series of waves and that each of these waves has a crest (top) and a trough (bottom). After gaining more experience in FOREX trading, it will become clear that tops and bottoms are considered to be major reversal patterns that signify a fundamental change in a long-term price trend. One of the most popular FOREX trading strategies is to attempt to detect a top or bottom and then trade to the next opposite one (i.e., enter at a top and trade to a bottom or enter at a bottom and trade to a top).

The main objective of traders who use this technique should

be to try and detect tops and bottoms as accurately as possible by using the techniques that will now be described. Scientific formulas such as the Elliot Wave, W D Gann or Fibonacci theories may be used. Each one is based on the theory that market behavior repeats itself. However, basing a strategy on such theories alone is not a wise practice and could put equity at risk.

One of the main reasons why these theories shouldn't be used on their own is that the FOREX market is not predictive in nature. The best any trader can hope for is to determine the probability of the market's next move. This means that, if you just try and predict the market's next move, you are, in fact, not playing the odds and, as such, will most likely lose. In addition, FOREX advances in a way that precludes the consistent prediction of prices. As a consequence, scientific theories should be used with caution and only in conjunction with other FOREX methods.

Other traders base their strategies on the favorite FOREX maxim, which is "buy low and sell high. However, this concept is not as easy to implement as it sounds. In order to detect a bottom, one must search for a support level against which price has bounced a number of times. Once achieved, an entry position can then be opened.

This activity is flawed in the sense that it involves guessing that the support will hold the next time. Obviously, guessing stacks the odds against a trader, inviting the possibility of failure.

To increase the chance of success, wait and confirm that the support will hold. Before entering a new trade, evidence that the support will remain intact and that the market has generated enough momentum to drive price back up is required.

The FOREX market is about odds rather than certainties. When this fact is understood, a trader can begin to position trades that are likely to achieve more wins than losses, which is the ultimate goal of any FOREX trader. A number of methods have been designed to aid in achieving these objectives.

One such method requires that a trader examine weekly and monthly charts in search of tops and bottoms. In particular, the key is to locate those top and bottoms against which the price has bounced a number of times. Once these tops and bottoms have been found, the peaks and troughs should be connected, creating resistance and supports lines for the currency pairs in question. These lines offer good chances of entering new trades on the rebound, especially if evidence of momentum buildup in the reverse direction is detected.

Another method commonly used to spot levels where reversals may take place is to locate psychological levels of currency pairs (e.g., 1.4000 for the EUR/USD). These numbers not only seem to have some kind of effect on the minds of traders, but also provide excellent opportunities for entry points. However, historical data should always be consulted in conjunction with this method in order to confirm that the levels held a number of times previously. Again, signs of reverse momentum need to be confirmed by setting the entry point about 20 PIPs back in the direction that the price is expected to reverse.

When searching for levels as described above, always remember that although the price may pierce through them, this action could be a fakeout and not a real breakout. To overcome this problem, employ a stop of about 100 PIPs. This will protect from fakeouts while opening up the possibility for an extremely large reward if a true breakout does occur.

Using a stop larger than 100 PIPs is discouraged because substantial losses may be suffered should a real fakeout occur. In addition, the stop should be moved to break even as soon as the price has reversed by 50 PIPs. This will keep you free of risk while giving the trade room to breathe.

Traders that find themselves in such enviable position must let their trades run in order to rake in big profits. Some of the most common top and bottom reversal patterns are discussed below. Detecting such patterns is a proven way to improve trading. As such, they should be studied carefully.

10.3.1 - Head and Shoulders Pattern

The famous head and shoulders pattern is formed by three peaks. The center peak, or head, is slightly higher than its two lower, and not necessarily symmetrical, shoulders. The line joining the bottoms of the two shoulders is called the neckline.

The neckline is rarely symmetrical or perfectly horizontal because of price fluctuations. This pattern is a strong reversal sign and is not complete until the neckline is broken. A good policy in order to confirm the momentum of the reversal is to wait for two successive closes below the neckline on the daily chart.

Some traders use the distance between the neckline and the top of the head to project a target level for their trade. They do this by measuring the distance from the neckline to the head in PIPs and then project the same distance below their entry point.

10.3.2 - Double Top and Bottom Patterns

Double top patterns, which are also called "M" patterns, are initially formed by a long rise in trading price. The shape then continues with two tops separated by a valley before terminating with a significant drop in the trade price.

Conversely, double bottom patterns are referred to as "W" patterns and commence with a long drop in currency price followed by two bottoms separated by a hill, ending with a sharp price rise. The main characteristics of top and bottom patterns are as follows:

1. Tops and bottoms are significant reversal patterns that usually mark the end of a long-term price trend.

2. Tops are usually more defined and shorter than bottoms.

3. The double top and bottom trends are strong indicators of a pending change in currency trading direction.

10.3.3 - Triple Top and Bottom Patterns

A triple top is a currency trading pattern where the price rebounds from its support level three times. A triple top is a very strong indication of a powerful resistance level.

Similarly, a triple bottom pattern occurs when the price retracts from its support level three times. Triple bottoms indicate a condition of very strong buying interest.

10.3.4 - V-Pattern

The V pattern is formed after a sharp price action switches very quickly from one direction to another without warning. In fact, trend reversals provide some of the best trading opportunities for opening positions that exhibit good profit potential. Reversals usually indicate major changes in the direction of currency pairs. However, after trading FOREX for a time it will become clear that a market top or bottom is often difficult to identify.

Traders are recommended to wait for prices to actually confirm a trend reversal by developing one of the above well-tested and reliable patterns. In summary, developing trading methods to enable the successful detection of tops and bottoms can be a very profitable activity. As such, it is well worth the time to become acquainted with these patterns.

10.4 – Experimenting with Technical Analysis

It should be clear at this point that a significant amount of experience is required before a novice can trade FOREX with well-designed stops and profit targets. Indeed, FOREX has such an unpredictable nature that it is easily capable of shutting down positions protected by just small stops (i.e., stops up to 50 PIPs).

In addition, FOREX trading is made all the more complex, especially for novices, because of the necessity to develop trading strategies that have good RR and win-loss ratios. However, achieving such positions will cost beginners both time and money if standard trading methods are utilized.

Do beginners have any plausible solutions? The answer is a resounding yes, especially if they design a well thought out trading strategy. For instance, the following strategy may at first appear very strange as its main concepts appear to contradict many of the recommended principles associated with FOREX trading. The strategy advises trading using a very large stop, somewhere on the order of 500 PIPs, while earning profits of around 50 PIPs per trade.

This idea could even be considered a macro version of the scalping strategy favored and employed by many FOREX robot designers. When scalping, the idea is to nip in and out of trades very quickly, both exposing the trader to minimum risk and earning very small profits of 5 to 10 PIPs. A strategy such as this is best applied when no fundamental news is scheduled for release.

It should be appreciated that a large stop of 500 PIPs is extremely difficult for even the FOREX to stop out. As such, this strategy provides beginners with a basis from which to trade because they no longer need the essential knowledge that is required to protect normal trades.

Of course, the RR ratio of 10:1 is appalling at first glance. However, the effort required on the part of the FOREX market to knock out a 500-PIP stop is exponentially higher than the effort required to close down a 50-PIP stop.

The idea is to achieve a very strong win-to-loss ratio, which will then offset the poor RR ratio. For instance, achieving 11 wins of 50 PIPs against 1 loss of 500 PIPs would result in a profit of 50 PIPs. Although this sounds good, the technique must be performed in the correct manner. If traders are not careful, then their trades could get marooned in negative territory. For example, price could stay within this region for months. If this were to happen, the possibility of registering a profit during this time effectively disappears.

To solve this problem, a very good money management strategy is required. Experts advise risking only 0.1 to 0.2 percent of total equity on any one trade. By doing this, the majority of one's equity is preserved should the 500-PIP stop be hit. In addition, traders will have the luxury of waiting for some time for marooned trades to drop back into profitable territory. Finally, by risking so little a number of trades may be opened at the same time.

The great advantage of this trading method is that it allows novices room to make mistakes that they would not enjoy if they continuously utilized small stops of 30 PIPs per trade. Beginners commonly argue that gaining 30- to 50-PIPs is a very small profit that would have a limited positive effect on equity. However, it should be realized that a successive wins result in exponential monetary growth, even if the targets are a small percentage of total equity.

Another problem arises when novices first exposed to this concept consider risking a larger percentage of their budget (e.g., 10 percent). They assume that they should be able to do this because they are using such a large stop.

Understand that this is definitely not a good idea, especially when it is considered that 10 successive losses using 10 percent risk per trade would consume 66% of a novice's total equity. In contrast, risking only 2 percent per trade would result in only 17.5 percent of total equity being lost should 10 consecutive losses occur. Clearly, the second case is far more desirable as it extends a novice's trading life and provides more equity protection. By applying the different trading methods outlined in this book, a novice can win many profitable trades against only a few losses.

Of course, no one becomes a FOREX expert overnight. In the same way that doctors and lawyers must hone their skills for years, so too must FOREX traders. As such, adopting a professional approach to using any and all trading strategies is the best way forward.

As previously mentioned, many experts advise evolving

a low-risk trading system into a high-risk strategy in small, incremental steps. This method is ideally suited to those attempting to utilize the large-stop strategy for the first time. The initial low-risk configuration of settings could consist of trading only one lot while using only 2 percent of total equity. Furthermore, only one currency pair will be traded at any time, and only one trade will be active at any one time.

Once success is achieved with a low-risk operational configuration, higher-risk strategies can be introduced by altering the settings one at a time. After a series of successful advancements, more than one lot can be traded and 10 percent of total equity may be used. Additionally, more than one currency pair will be traded and more than one trade can be active at any given time.

This methodology allows for experimentation in small increments of risk and avoids a situation where traders jump into a new trading situation before gaining the proper experience. The concepts discussed below can also enhance a trader's chances of seeing increased profitability.

1. If possible, always try to trade with the trend. This is the equivalent of swimming with the tide.

2. Use processes that will help distinguish fakeouts from very profitable true breakouts.

3. Consider moving the stop loss to break even after a suitable profit has been recorded. This allows for the experience of risk-free trading.

4. Remember to aim for small profits of about 50 PIPs. Do not forget that a successive number of small wins will produce an exponential rise in equity.

5. Finally, do not attempt to trade the large-stop strategy when major fundamental news releases are scheduled. These events can increase volatility considerably, resulting

in large, random price movements.

One of the main features of this strategy is that it does not involved trying to achieve a profit of 500 percent per month. In fact, very few trading strategies are capable of producing such returns. Instead, if performed correctly, this strategy promises small returns while offering novices the time to learn and develop a professional feel for FOREX.

This large stop-loss strategy also provides the opportunity to profit from the carry trade [26]. This can be accomplished by selling a currency with a low interest rate and purchasing another posting at a higher interest rate. For instance, if a trade goes against you, taking advantage of the carry trade will still allow you to recoup some, if not all, of your potential losses.

10.5 – How to Develop a Breakout Strategy

One of the most popular FOREX strategies consists of trading breakouts. The strategy is easy to implement and can produce excellent results. The main edict of this trading method states that if a currency pair has been trading for some time within a tight range, when it does breakout it usually proceeds to move in the same direction for some time.

As such, the initial step in designing a breakout strategy is to locate a method that will readily identify currency pairs that have been trading within a tight range for a period of time using technical analysis. Once this is achieved, potential entry conditions can then be determined and eventually activated when the breakout occurs.

Although breakout trading can be applied to any currency pair, it should only be applied to the major currency pairs. This is because one can more readily study the patterns of major pairs and thus develop an appreciation of their movements.

The tight trading range of a currency pair is confined by a ceiling or resistance level and a floor or support level. Very often, a price will bounce against its ceiling or floor a number of times before it finally bursts out. For example, assume the EUR/USD has bounced off its resistance level at 1.3800 a number of times. An eventual breach of this level is a very strong indication that opening a long trade should be considered.

A very good policy is to monitor for breakouts using technical analysis. When doing so, use longer time frames as they produce more accurate statistics (i.e., daily and upwards). In addition, it is best to wait until the close of the selected time period during which the breakout occurs. This will provide enough time to confirm that the breakout is real.

The drawback to using this technique is that the price may keep rising dramatically and even approach the intended target before the close of the period. If this does happen, a new trade should not be activated. More frequently, if a trader does not apply patience and wait for the period close, the possibility of profit could be lost due to a false signal or fakeout.

When a trade does close significantly above the breakout level, a retraction frequently occurs, which pulls the price back to the original breakout level before it proceeds in the direction of the breakout. There is much speculation that this effect is actually caused by large banking institutions forcing these types of conditions deliberately in order to stop out smaller players.

In such cases, traders should place an entry order at the original breakout point with a stop of about 50 PIPs. By doing so, they can quite frequently capture a more profitable breakout position at less risk. Always keep RR and win-to-loss ratios in mind and seek better trading positions should the opportunities arise.

A good breakout strategy works best when it is incorporated with technical features such as resistance, support and pivot points, as well as technical patterns such as flags, pennants and head and shoulders). One of the prime reasons that traders like to use a breakout strategy is that it provides them with the opportunity of entering a trade at the earliest signs of a new trend or price channel development. This is a very lucrative and low-risk position to capture because these positions can be the starting points of major price movements.

As stated before, a breakout occurs when a currency price breaches either the support or resistance levels of a tight trading range. The increased volatility that provides the momentum for the price to achieve this breakout is usually capable of propelling it further in the breakout direction for some time. When this happens, a new price channel has been created.

The most powerful breakout events occur when the price pattern emerges from technical patterns such as flags or pennants. Every trader (i.e., intraday, daily or weekly) should understand this concept.

The best breakout candidates can usually be identified by detecting the conditions described below. As price bounced off its support or resistance a number of times, determine if the trading pattern formed a flag or a pennant formation. If so, the price will need to develop large amounts of momentum to force a breakout that may generate further price movements in the same direction.

Entry points for breakout trading are very easy to determine. Wait for the close of the time period containing the breakout and then set an entry just above the original resistance for a bull position or below the original support for a bear position.

Take care to distinguish a true breakout from a fakeout. A fakeout occurs when the price breaks, only to finish trading back within the original tight trading constraint at the day's end. This is why it is so important to confirm a positive close at the end of the current trading period before taking action.

If a trader acts too quickly, there is no guarantee that the price momentum will be sustained. This is why many traders also look for other signs, such as an increase in volatility, in order to confirm a real breakout. In addition, a good exit plan should be devised before embarking on a new breakout trade. One technique traders often use is to consult recent trading patterns of the currency pair in question. This allows them to determine a realistic target by calculating, for example, the average of recent price swings.

Equally important is planning an exit should the trade fail. it helps to know that an old resistance becomes the new support in a bull breakout, while an old support becomes the new resistance in a bear breakout. Using this information, traders can locate a good position for a stop by placing either below the new support lever or above the new resistance level.

Should the trade settle back within its old trading range, then the breakout has failed and an exit route should be immediately considered. A suitably positioned stop will allow you to do this which you need to select at trade entry. It is very important to accept the loss as quickly as possible and not allow it to grow into a monster.

For bull runs, many traders place their stops 50 PIPs below the original resistance. Similarly, they place stops 50 PIPs above the original support for bear positions. Below is a summary of actions to be taken when trading breakouts. Note that any strategy used should allow the trader to perform each of these tasks with confidence.

1. First, identify suitable currency pairs that are prime breakout candidates. Search for pairs that have been trading in a tight range for some time. Preferably, locate those that have formed clear trading patterns such as flags or pennants.

2. Look for strong resistance and support levels that the price has bounced against a number of times. This implies that the currency pair contains a large amount of pent-up energy waiting for release. In this instance, a currency pair may be likened to a volcano on the verge of erupting.

3. Wait for the breakout to occur. Once this event happens, confirm the breakout's real intentions by waiting for

the close of the time period within which the breakout occurred. This will help guard against fakeouts.

4. Before entering the trade, select an achievable exit target by using a method such as calculating the average movements from historical data under similar conditions.

It should be noted that very often the trade will retest its old resistance or support levels before proceeding further. Traders should be prepared for this mentally. If the levels hold, a new price channel may well be formed. If not, a fakeout could occur. At this point, one should exit using a predetermined stop strategy. If, after a day or so, no clear confirmation of the breakout has materialized, traders should consider closing their positions, preferably without loss, and moving onto the next opportunity.

Breakout trading requires patience, and a good plan should ideally remove emotions from the equation. This is because the market needs to generate considerable amounts of volatility to force a breakout. Afterwards, price movements can move rapidly, resulting in many traders becoming over-excited. As discussed previously, emotions can impair judgment and lead to financial loss.

A good breakout strategy must keep traders emotionally detached during these events, allowing them to trade professionally toward achievable targets while keeping them at minimum risk. Finally, you're a new breakout strategy should be tested thoroughly before using it during live trading. This can be done by calculating the strategy's expectancy value and win-to-loss ratio.

Use historical data for the chosen currency pairs before advancing onto demo trading or live trading using small monetary values. Designing a profitable breakout strategy takes time, but many successful FOREX traders have found that the effort is well worth it.

10.6 - Trend Retracements Using Technical Analysis

Another very popular FOREX strategy is trend retracements. The major advantage of this strategy is that using allows experts and novices alike to trade with the trend. However, one must first determine whether a price is performing a retracement or undergoing a major reversal. This distinction is very important because it will provide insight into whether a price decline is long-term or a mere relief dip.

For instance, many traders have experienced the frustrations caused when they have closed positions prematurely, only to watch price then accelerate in its original direction. To overcome this major drawback, it is important to identify and trade retracements properly.

What exactly are retracements? They are temporary price reversals that occur within a larger price trend or channel. The most important feature of a retracement is that it does not last for any great length of time before the trend resumes in its original direction. Traders should know how to distinguish retracements from more serious and long-term reversals. There are a number of main differences between retracements and reversals that will assist in their identification:

1. Retracements are usually caused by small traders taking profits and as such do not produce large increases in trading volume. Full reversals are normally driven by large institutional selling and generate significant increases in trading volume.

2. Retracements produce few serious chart patterns and the ones they do produce are mainly limited to a few minor candlestick patterns. Reversals, on the other hand, are very serious events and are capable of producing major chart formations such as double top or head and shoulders patterns.

3. The lifespan of a retracement is usually very short and

normally lasts no longer than a week or two at the most. Reversals, on the other hand, are more permanent events that may last for weeks or even months.

4. Retracements are born normally after large price movements have occurred, while reversals can occur at any time.

Why is it so important to distinguish between these two events? Traders will always have to contend with difficult choices — such as determining whether to hold a trade open and risk serious loss — whenever price reversals take place.

Alternately, a trader may sell at the first sign of a price drop and then re-buy at a more favorable discount. However, the risk of losing larger gains by doing so is certainly present should the price suddenly surge back in its original direction.

Another choice is simply closing the trade completely, but a serious profit opportunity may be lost if price makes a full recovery and more. In short, a method must be devised that will allow for the detection of retracements and the determination of their scopes. The most popular tools for undertaking this task are as follows:

1. Fibonacci retracements [27]
2. Trendline support and resistance levels
3. Support, resistance and pivot point levels

Fibonacci retracements are percent values that can be used to forecast the levels of corrections in a trending market. The most popular retracement levels are 38.2 percent, 50 percent and 61.8 percent.

In a strong trend, a trader can anticipate the price to retract by 38.2 percent. In contrast, weaker trends can generate corrections closer to 61.8 percent. The 50-percent mark is a good place to sell in downtrends or buy in uptrends.

Trends create price channels that have an upper boundary (or upper trendline) and a lower boundary (or lower trendline). Retracements always bounce off these trendlines before price resumes moving in its original direction. A full reversal, however, will break through a trendline.

Pivot points can also be utilized to detect important resistance and support levels. A pivot point and its associated supports and resistances are levels at which the direction of price can possibly change. For example, pivot points can be used to recognize key levels that need to be broken for a move to be classified as a real breakout.

It should be understood that a retracement can quickly change into a full-blown reversal without warning. To protect against serious loss, traders must devise a sensible stop-loss strategy. To accomplish this, place stops just below the long-term trendline support if long, and just above the long-term resistance trendline if short.

Upon locating methods to aid in distinguishing a retracement from a reversal and determining scope, a trend retracement trading strategy must be devised. A breakout strategy may well be used to help define the birth of new price trends or channels. Afterwards, you can then look for retracements to help determine low-risk trade entries that have good potential profits.

Once a trend drops to one of its trendlines, consider activating a trade entry. A protective stop may also be set on the other side of the trendline to protect from a full reversal. If you are unable to clearly see a trending channel on the chart of a particular currency pair, leave it and study others. To be successful at this type of trading, a clearly defined trading pattern must be identified.

Remember to avoid activating a trade in a trend that is just forming as it may be a fakeout. Similarly, be careful if a trend has been in existence for some time as it may be coming to the end of its life. In addition, do not apply this technique during times when major fundamental releases are imminent because of the potential they have for creating high levels of volatility.

Another way to look at trends is to realize that they are produced from collective human emotions. This is known as sentiment in market terms. Retracements are sometimes created because sentiment has driven the trend too far in one direction, producing the need for a potential correction.

As stated above, one of the best ways to determine how far a price retracement will reverse before turning back in the direction of the trend is to use Fibonacci retracement levels. The most common Fibonacci levels that are used by traders are 38.2 percent, 50 percent, and 61.8 percent of a trend.

These are the expected levels that the currency price will revert back to during a retracement. If the level holds and an entry point can be created, a trade with an excellent RR ratio can be activated. Indeed, many traders activate trades at one Fibonacci level while placing their stops on the over side of the next level (e.g., buy at 38.2 percent with a stop on the over side of 50 percent).

Although this is a good way of defining entry points, Fibonacci levels are not an exact science and can be very misleading to traders, especially novices. Many times, traders become too impatient and enter trades before the trend has actually formed. They also have a tendency to assume, for example, that the 38.2-percent Fibonacci level will hold without allowing enough time to monitor exactly what the market will do.

The assimilation of the above information is tantamount to protection from these problems. It is important to be patient and wait until the end of the closing period in question as a means of allowing enough time to evaluate the position accurately. In conclusion, it can be said that traders who have gained a sufficient amount of experience trading FOREX understand that a strategy based on trend retracements provides excellent opportunities for profit by locating low-risk re-entry points.

11

Technical Indicators

Technical Indicators

A number of very popular technical indicators were introduced in Chapter 6. This chapter will go a step further by describing the concepts behind a number of widely used indicators together with advice concerning their best usage.

11.1 - Bollinger Bands

John Bollinger invented Bollinger bands during the early part of the 1980s. He identified a requirement for adaptive trading bands after he concluded that volatility possessed a dynamic nature as opposed to a static one, as was the common perception at that time. Bollinger bands can be used to better understand how the high and low prices of a currency pair interact with each other. A main feature of this technical indicator is that price achieves high values at the upper band and low values at the lower band.

Consequently, Bollinger bands can assist in making quality trading decisions by enabling a comparison of price action to the signals produced by other technical indicators. From the trading chart below, it should be clear that Bollinger Bands care comprised of three curves (blue lines) that track the movements of the currency pair. The central band is an SMA that acts as the base for the upper and lower bands while at the same time displaying the intermediate-term trend.

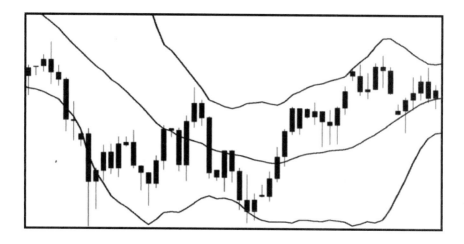

The distance between the bands is determined by the level of volatility and standard deviation of the same data that was used to determine the middle band. The default values of the two standard deviations can be tweaked, if required.

Bollinger bands are generally used to evaluate the present volatility of price, because Bollinger bands can indicate whether price is experiencing high or low volatility. For example, the bands narrow when price movements are small, but increase in distance when price generates higher levels of volatility. These features can be clearly seen in the above chart.

Notice that the bands shrink in the middle of the diagram when price adopts a range trending pattern. Both to the left and right of this pattern, it should also be apparent that the bands are wider in distance because price is moving in trends.

Traders who focus on these attributes are very adept at using Bollinger bands. It is not necessary to understand how Bollinger bands are calculated. However, a trader should be acutely aware that price has a strong tendency to always oscillate about the middle band.

By looking at the above chart, it can be seen that this oscillation happened a number of times. Essentially, the upper band acts as a resistance level while the lower band acts as a support level. Consequently, price often bounces off these two bands.

As you might guess, better results will be achieved using the Bollinger bands if they are displayed on trading charts utilizing the daily time frame or higher. Many traders have field-tested good trading strategies that can be constructed using Bollinger bands. However, it should be cautioned that Bollinger bands perform best when price is range trading.

11.2 - Elliot Wave Oscillator

This oscillator has been designed using the Elliot wave theory, which specifies that a price trend is usually represented by a three- or five-wave sequence of advances or declines. The waves are mainly generated by crowd psychology. Again, greater chances of success are possible if this oscillator is displayed on trading charts using the daily time frame or higher.

In order to utilize the Elliot Wave Oscillator [29], a currency pair that is advancing in a five-wave pattern must be detected. Once accomplished, it must be confirmed that price achieved a peak value at the top of wave three before it started to reverse. If this is so, then this is a definite sign that a retracement has commenced that will comprise three further waves.

If it can also be determined that a wave bounces against a Fibonacci support or resistance level, then a price reversal is imminent. Indeed, Elliot's wave theory has been verified by an extensive range of tools and trading strategies. The Elliot wave oscillator was developed using the observations that currency pairs tend to advance in five- and three-wave patterns and that major changes in price direction coincide with Fibonacci support and resistance levels.

In fact, a number of trading strategies based on the combined attributes of Elliott waves and Fibonacci retracements already exist. Experts will advise that the price patterns associated with these two theories often repeat themselves on trading charts.

However, a good education in all aspects of FOREX trading is required before being able to fully understand and utilize the Elliot wave oscillator.

However, a trader's research should not be restricted to technical analysis alone, but should also include risk and money management. One must know how to control risks in order to use the Elliot Wave Oscillator Without the possibility of incurring significant financial losses. This oscillator can be used to locate price formations such as tops and bottoms on the trading charts of currency pairs of interest.

The basic premise of the Elliot wave oscillator is that trading sentiment fluctuates from optimism to pessimism in a natural sequence that creates waves in price movements. These oscillations produce the patterns that are illustrated in the following chart.

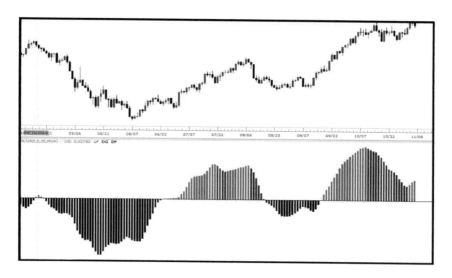

The Elliott wave oscillator is presented as a histogram that represents a 35-period moving price average that is subtracted from a 5-period moving price average. As the above diagram illustrates, this histogram fluctuates above and below a zero line. The Elliot wave oscillator can assist traders perform the following tasks:

1. Minimizing losses if price reverses direction quickly
2. Deducing when the next price correction is due
3. Quickly determining if a long or short trade should be opened
4. Accurately forecasting when trends will terminate

11.3 - Fibonacci Retracements

Traders who need to forecast the future price direction of a currency pair may utilize the Fibonacci retracement to this end. Indeed, the Fibonacci retracement is a top technical indicator that can be used to trade various markets, including stocks, FOREX, commodities and futures. This section explains Fibonacci retracements and describes the best methods available for using this powerful technical indicator.

Retracements were first discovered by Leonardo Fibonacci in the 12th century. He suggested that price will retrace by a predetermined percentage of its entire latest movement before it proceeds in its initial direction. The percentages are 61.8 percent, 50.0 percent, and 38.2 percent. Interestingly enough, Leonardo detected these ratios when he noticed that a person's belly button is located at precisely 61.8 percent of the distance between the feet and head. In addition, you're a person's elbow is positioned at 61.8 percent of the distance between their shoulder and hand. There are numerous other examples of this interesting rule in nature.

Can these facts assist in trading FOREX? Yes, because Fibonacci retracements also relate strongly to the price movements of currency pairs.

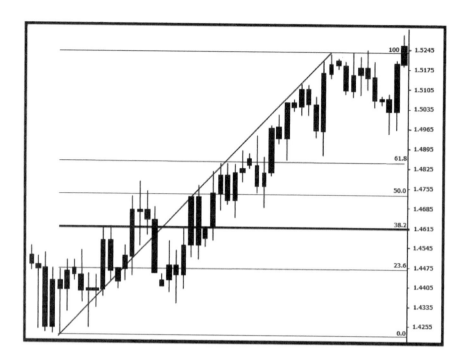

For instance, notice the red line drawn from the bottom to the top of the bull trend on the right of the above chart. The displayed Fibonacci retracements can be used to determine how far price is anticipated to retract before advancing again in its initial direction.

Fundamentally, when using this indicator, it is important to locate trading charts that are displaying the largest possible price trends. A line must then be drawn connecting the trough to the peak, as shown by the red line in the above diagram. Your trading platform can then generate the Fibonacci retracements automatically to produce lines similar to the blue ones in the above chart.

The three most important blue lines depict the retracement distances that are equal to 38.2 percent, 50 percent and 61.8 percent of the total initial price movement that is represented by the red line. For example, the 50-percent retracement represents the level to which price will retract if it has reversed by 50 percent of the total distance of its initial bull movement.

If the currency pair retreats to one of the Fibonacci retracements, then this is a good signal to open a new position in the direction of the original price movement. For instance, if price bounces against the 61.2-percent retracement in the above diagram, then this development should be regarded as a strong buy signal. If a new buy trade is opened, then the stop should be located just below the next Fibonacci level which, in this case, is the 50-percent mark.

11.4 - Commodity Channel Index

The Commodity Channel Index (CCI) [30], invented by Donald Lambert, can be used to help detect cyclical movements in price. Lambert founded the construction of his CCI on the idea that currency pairs, commodities and stocks always progress in cycles, with highs and lows occurring at periodic intervals.

He initially recommended using a third of a complete cycle as the maximum time for the CCI. For instance, if using a 60-day cycle, the CCI will provide the best results if a time frame of 20 days is selected.

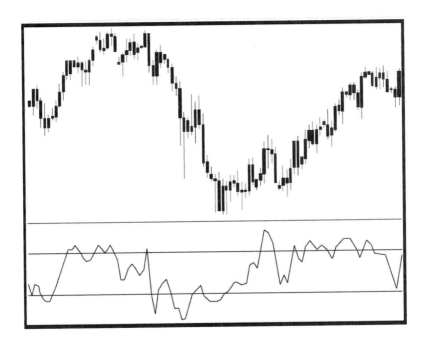

It needs to be appreciated that a buy signal is generated by the CCI if it records a reading that has just bounced above its -100 value. Similarly, a sell sign is produced when the CCI drops below its +100 value. These two important levels are displayed by the red horizontal lines in the above chart.

Novices need to know that 70 to 80 percent of all CCI values are produced between +100 and -100. This means that sell and buy signals are produced only about 20 to 30 percent of the time. For example, if a trader detects price forming a strong uptrend and a new buy position is opened after the CCI advances above its -100 value. The position should only be closed after the CCI reverses back below its +100 value.

Similarly, experts advise selling when the CCI falls below +100 and closing after the CCI moves back above -100. If the above chart is examined in light of these considerations, a number of very good selling and buying opportunities should be apparent.

The CCI can also be used to assist in the identification of price reversals. This can be accomplished by understanding that price is deemed to be oversold when the CCI drops below -100 and overbought when it registers readings above +100. A new buy signal may also be provided after the CCI climbs back above -100 from oversold levels. Similarly, a sell signal will be generated when the CCI falls back below +100 from overbought levels. Divergences can also be used to improve the quality of the CCI signal.

Consequently, the CCI should be used to assist in detecting trend strength, price reversals and price extremes. However, experts will advise that the CCI is best used in conjunction with other technical indicators. The CCI is classified as a momentum oscillator.

11.5 - The DeMarker Indicator

The DeMarker indicator (DI) [31] can be used to detect new trading opportunities because its designer, Tom DeMarker, invented it with this task specifically in mind. Traders find that the DI has many features that are similar to those of technical indicators produced by Welles Wilder. This is because DeMarker attempted to address the many serious problems related to identifying oversold and overbought conditions inherent in FOREX tools and strategies of the time.

Fundamentally, the DI monitors the sentiment of traders as it relates to currency pairs. This indicator does so by comparing the present value of a currency pair to that of a previous identified time period. Consequently, the DI can be used to judge traders' interest in a currency pair. This piece of information could very possibly assist in detecting tops and bottoms.

It should be noted that the DI makes no attempt to filter its data. Consequently, this indicator can also be used to detect new quality trading opportunities. Two variants of the DI exist, although they both use the same principles. The first one has a range that operates between -100 and +100, while the second fluctuates between 0 and 1. The next chart illustrates the second variant.

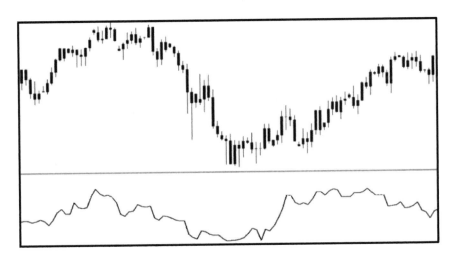

If the second variant is used, then it should be understood that values above 0.7 should be viewed as price tops and potential bear reversals, while values below 0.3 forecast market bottoms. If detecting readings between 0.3 and 0.7, consider that price is range trading. These features can be easily identified in the above chart.

The attributes of the DI can also be used to identify new quality trading opportunities. For example, a look at the above chart should reveal that the DI rises above its 0.3 value about midway, forming a new bull trend. The DI has acquired a good reputation for recognizing the birth of new trends and new trading opportunities.

It should also be appreciated that the DI is a very good tool for distinguishing between fakeouts and breakouts. This is because the design of the DI makes it very effective at identifying real price reversals, especially on intra-day charts and above.

The DI calculates the difference between the present price value and that of the previous time period. The figure is then stored by the DI if a positive result is achieved. If not, it is zeroed. The sum of all these values over a chosen time period is then divided by the lowest price value that was registered in the sequence.

As mentioned, DeMarker also recommended that his technical indicator be used to forecast price reversal patterns such as tops and bottoms. Interestingly, the DI has acquired such a good track record that many traders use it on its own to help them detect new trading opportunities.

11.6 - The Money Flow Index (MFI)

Traders have benefitted greatly by incorporating the many attributes of the money flow index (MFI) [32] into their trading strategies. This is especially true if a trader enjoys using technical analysis to study FOREX. The MFI can be exploited to quantify the sums of money flowing into and out of currency pairs of interest.

The MFI has many features that exhibit numerous similarities to those of the popular and well-known RSI. However, the RSI was invented to monitor volume, whereas the MFI tracks price. Colin Twiggs developed the MFI by basing it on the concepts of an early technical indicator invented by Marc Chaikin.

Twiggs advised that the MFI be used to help detect the births and terminations of trends. Again, the MFI generates better quality statistics when it is displayed on trading charts using the daily time frame and higher. Additionally, traders are recommended to verify all MFI findings by utilizing a second confirmatory technical indicator.

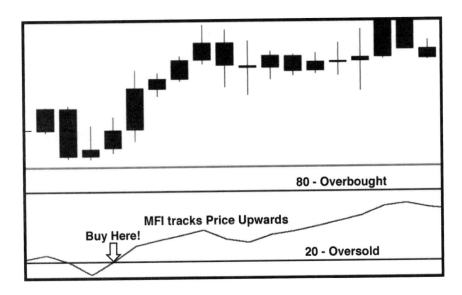

If the MFI is beginning to retract from its oversold level at 20 and starts tracking a rising price action, then this is a good signal that a new bull trend has been created. Similarly, good quality selling opportunities can be identified if the MFI drops below its overbought level at 80 and supports decreasing values in price.

For instance, in the above diagram it can be seen that the MFI (blue line) is indicating a good entry point for a buy trade. To be able to utilize the MFI well, one must realize that it signals overbought conditions for the currency pair when it produces readings of 80 or more, as in the chart above. Similarly, values of 20 or less are viewed as oversold conditions.

For example, if the MFI has just climbed above its 20th

level after recording oversold values, then a trader must consider such a development as a strong buying opportunity. Under such circumstances, caution is still advised because price may still plunge by hundreds of PIPs. Consequently, one should always confirm all MFI readings by using a secondary technical indicator before opening a new position.

The RSI may be used as a confirmation backup. If any serious disparities are produced after using these two indicators, consider delaying any further action until clarification clearer understanding of the situation develops. For instance, if the RSI is suggesting that the price is still rising but the MFI values are dropping, one should only consider opening a new trade once the two indicators' signals begin to align.

Please note that the MFI generates its readings by multiplying volume by the average price and then ranging the results on a scale between 100 and 0. If the MFI is starting to post a falling reading but price is still climbing, it's likely that a new market top is forming.

It is recommended to use the MFI as follows to identify good quality trading opportunities. Selling opportunities can be determined after the MFI attains readings above 80 but then begins to retract below this level. Conversely, buys can be determined when the MFI readings climbing back above its oversold level at 20. In addition, if the MFI values and price are starting to diverge, a change in the direction of the currency pair of interest may be imminent.

11.7 - The On Balance Volume Indicator

The on balance volume indicator (OBV) [33] can be used to compare the price and volume flows of a currency pair over a chosen time period. Joseph E. Granville invented the OBV in 1962 and introduced it to the markets together with his OBV theory in the book How to Read the Stock Market. The OBV has gained a reputation as one of the most famous momentum indicators that can be used to determine the relationships among volume, price and the momentum of stocks, commodities, futures and currency pairs.

The OBV regards all of a trading day's volume as up-volume if the price of a currency pair registers a higher daily close than its previous reading. Alternately, the OBV will classify a day's volumes as down volume if price posts a closing value that is lower than that of the previous day's closing. Consequently, the OBV line represents the cumulative total of all these negative and positive volume flows.

The above features can be observed in the diagram below. Note that the OBV may be predicting an imminent price retracement when its values begin to change course. In fact, it was Granville himself who first identified this important attribute of his invention. In the diagram below, the OBV starts to fall, announcing the end of the present bull trend.

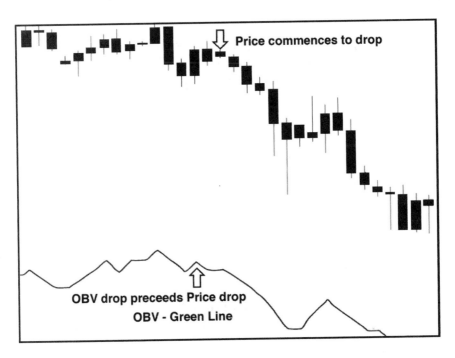

If the OBV readings are climbing, price should have started to climb as well. The OBV can also assist in the detection of new trends. For instance, if the OBV starts to produce a sequence of higher peaks and troughs, such a development can be viewed as a good quality buy signal. Alternately, if the OBV begins posting a series of lower tops and dips, then this pattern can be interpreted as a very strong sell signal.

The development of new quality trading opportunities can also be determined if the OBV begins to generate values that diverge from price. This is because the design of the OBV focuses on the trends of currency pairs. Granville recommended that if volume starts to decrease during a bull trend, then a market top may be forming as buying pressure has begun to fade. If you observe such a development, expect a retraction very soon. Granville also verified that a similar action occurs in bear trends if volume begins to increase.

In addition to the above points, Granville also recommended using a 20-period moving average in conjunction with his OBV in order to help detect when trends are about to terminate. Such events are more easily detected by identifying the crossovers of the moving average and the OBV. Indeed, the OBV is one of the simplest and most popular of all the momentum indicators.

Price reversals may also be due when divergences are noticed between the OBV and price. If the OBV is also altering direction after it has been following price for some time, then this development should be viewed as a possible new trading opportunity.

11.8 - Directional Movement Index

The Directional Movement Index (DMI) [34] can be an excellent tool for evaluating price direction and strength. Welles Wilde, who also invented the famous RSI, designed and released the DMI in 1978. The DMI should be used to help traders decide whether to trade short or long.

The DMI is extremely effective at distinguishing between weak and strong price trends. Consequently, experts advise on integrating the DMI into trend trading strategies because it will aid in the detection of the strongest trends.

The DMI has a very adaptable design that enables it to function well with most time frames. The DMI can also be used to track all types of investments, including commodities, stocks, futures and currencies. The following chart illustrates some of the main attributes of the DMI and demonstrates how it can be used to increase profits when trading FOREX.

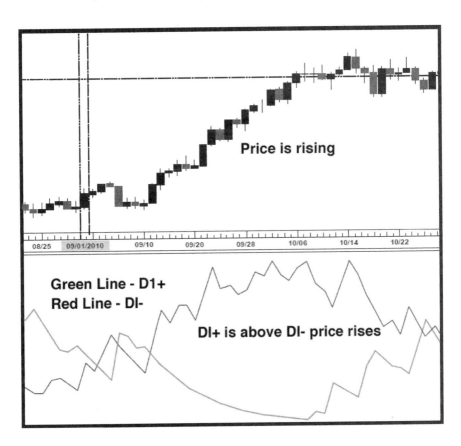

The DMI is a moving average that is normally used with a default time period of 14. The positive directional movement indicator (DI+) displays the power of price to climb upwards (the green line in the above chart), while the negative directional movement indicator (DI-) represents the ability of price to move downward (the red line in the above chart).

A trader's first task when studying the DMI is to determine which of the two DI lines is above the other and in ascendency. The one that is at the top is termed the dominant DI and will normally indicate the current direction of price. Necessarily, for and sellers to switch dominance the two lines must execute a crossover.

For example, it can be seen in the above chart that the DI+ climbs above the DI-, heralding a new bull trend. Note that price follows as well by climbing in unison. Although a crossover is registered when the DI+ climbs above the DI-, caution should still be exercised because these crossovers are not definite buy or sell signals. As such, traders should use a second indicator to confirm any recommendations provided by the DMI.

DMI crossovers can often be misleading because they can frequently generate false signals when volatility is low and produce delayed signals when volatility is high. DMI crossovers should therefore be regarded as a first sign that a change in the direction of price could be imminent.

The DMI can be used to trade both trending and range-bound currency pairs. Either of these tasks can be accomplished by understanding that price is trending downwards when the DI- is above the DI+, while a bullish price action is dominating when the DI+ line is above the DI- line.

11.9 - True Strength Index (TSI)

The true strength index (TSI) [35] can be used to determine when a currency pair can be classified as either overbought or oversold. The TSI is similar in many regards to the popular RSI because both function as momentum indicators.

The readings produced by the TSI result from studying the short-term purchasing momentum of a currency pair over a specified time period. In addition, the design of the TSI is essentially an attempt at conquering the standard lagging issues associated with most moving average technical indicators.

Consequently, the TSI is more sensitive to the existing trading conditions of a currency pair than the RSI because of its improved design. This enhanced performance is evident in the trading chart below, which compares the TSI and the RSI.

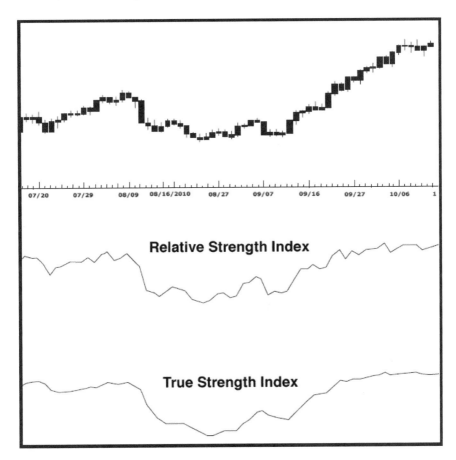

It should also be noted that the TSI was designed to produce accurate readings with minimum time lag while at the same time monitoring price. Consequently, if the TSI starts to generate readings that are increasing in value, then this development is usually complemented by a rise in the price of the currency pair of interest.

Conversely, if the TSI begins to post decreasing values, price will also start to fall. Examples of both of these conditions can be seen in the above diagram.

Note that the TSI's ability to aid in the identification of oversold and overbought conditions of currency pairs is possible because of two main features:

1. The TSI tracks the short-term buying momentum of currency pairs.

2. The TSI makes use of the lagging property of moving averages.

In addition, traders working with the TSI will begin to understand that a 25-day exponential moving average is first added to the difference between price bars. The result is then added to a 13-day EMA to create the TSI readings. The TSI advises that price is overbought when it produces values of 25 or more, while it indicates oversold states when it registers values of 25 or less.

As the TSI is a variation of the RSI, its oversold and overbought features to those of the RSI. As mentioned previously, this task can be performed by analyzing the above diagram.

In conclusion, it can be asserted that the TSI can be utilized to detect new trading opportunities. As illustrated in the above diagram, if TSI readings drop and close below its overbought level of 25, then such developments may be regarded as selling opportunities. Similarly, if TSI values are observed to climb and close above the -25 level, then this can be considered a buying opportunity.

12

Designing a Customized Trading Strategy

Designing a Customized
Trading Strategy

The previous chapters of this book have introduced many of the main aspects of FOREX trading. This chapter will now discuss developing a trading strategy by using a series of easy-to-follow steps. A new trading strategy should be based on the following considerations:

1. Every trader needs a technique that will allow for the identification of good quality trading opportunities that display minimum risk and excellent profit potential.

2. An exit strategy must be designed in order to maximize profits.

3. Any viable strategy must allow a trader to distinguish between fakeouts and real trading opportunities.

If the foundation of a trading strategy can be built on the above points, a trader's chances of profiting from FOREX will be greatly increased. The following steps will help to define strategies that will be compliant with the three important concepts described above.

12.1 – Selecting the Optimum Time Frame

Traders must first determine how much available time they have daily to trade FOREX. For example, a considerable portion of daily time is needed to monitor open positions if a trader intends to utilize strategies such as scalping, which often uses time frames of 1, 5, 15 and 30 minutes.

Novices are strongly advised to base their strategies on the longer time frames (i.e., daily and upwards). A beginner can then make use of the superior statistics that are associated with longer time frames. As mentioned, this can more easily aid in the identification of price formations. Consequently, a trader will be able to better define risks and therefore ensure maximum equity protection.

12.2 – Choosing Technical Indicators

As described earlier in the book, there is a vast array of technical indicators from which to choose. Novices should experiment with technical indicators in order to determine which ones produce the best quality trading opportunities. This task can be accomplished by adjusting the key parameters of each preferred technical indicator using a demo account.

After each test, reevaluate the performance of each technical indicator by calculating the new win-to-loss ratio and expectancy value of the trading strategy. When building a strategy completely from scratch, a significant amount of time may be needed to adequately perform these steps.

12.3 – Which Currency Pair to Trade?

Traders quickly realize that each currency pair possesses its own trading dynamics and behavioral patterns. Consequently, novices are advised to trade the EUR/USD currency pair to begin with until more experience is gained. In this way, novices will be able to take advantage of the currency pairs numerous positive attributes, which include its constant high liquidity and low spreads. It should be noted that nearly 80% of all FOREX transactions include the EUR/USD currency pair.

The Euro is regarded as the base currency of this pair while the USD is considered the counter or quote. As such, if the EUR/USD is quoted at 1.4000, then you can exchange US$1.400 for each Euro.

If one can predict in which direction the EUR/USD will next move, profits can be realized. For instance, if it is forecasted that the Euro will fall against the US Dollar, then a trader should sell the EUR/USD. For example, assume that a trader has just sold the EUR/USD at 1.3800. If the exchange rate then plunges to 1.3500, the trader makes a 300-PIP profit.

A FOREX broker will charge a fee, in the form of a spread, every time a new trade is activated. The spread of a currency pair is the difference between its buy and sell prices. Consequently, novices are always recommended to identify a good FOREX broker who can constantly supply the lowest spreads possible because this cost can obviously restrict a trader's profits. A beginner should also choose to trade those currency pairs that display the lowest spreads. The EUR/USD is always a good selection because it exhibits one of the smallest spreads possible.

Attempting to trade other currency pairs possessing wider spreads will make achieving consistent profits a much harder task. For example, if the present spread of a currency pair is 6 PIPs, then a trader must gain a profit of this value just to break even. Under such circumstances, a broker's commission will be the 6 PIPs. This is one of the main reasons why beginners are recommended to trade the EUR/USD. This currency pair's spreads normally hover in the region of 3 PIPs. In contrast, other more exotic currency pairs have spreads that can be in excess of 15 PIPs.

The EUR/USD also enjoys high liquidity. This is an important attribute because it always provides a trader with the ability to open positions given the fact that other traders will be present to support these transactions. As such, experts recommend that novices acquire or design a trading strategy that will allow them to take advantage of the many positive attributes of the EUR/USD currency pair.

12.4 – Designing a Confirmation Strategy

Once the first three steps have been completed, you will have constructed a basic strategy based on preferred time frames, technical indicators and currency pairs. At this point, good quality trading opportunities possessing minimum risk and optimum profit can be identified.

However, equity must now be safeguarded further by providing increased protection against fakeouts or false signals. This task can be accomplished by designing a confirmation technique that can then be integrated into the trading strategy. Experts recommend that this objective be satisfied by investigating other technical indicators that can verify the results of your primary indicator. Under no circumstances should this step be omitted as it will provide additional equity protection.

Select a secondary technical indicator that complies with the objectives of your strategy. Indeed, this is one of the prime reasons why Chapter 11 contains an in-depth analysis of these tools. In addition, Section 10.2 explains why so many experts utilize candlestick technology to help them verify all the recommendations produced by their primary technical indicators. Chapter 11 and Section 10.2 should be consulted when choosing a secondary technical indicator.

12.5 – Controlling Risks

Put simply, controlling risks is an aspect of trading that cannot be ignored. If traders do not introduce measures to restrict your risk levels, their chances of survival are slim. Devise a simple money management strategy that allows for a precise determination of the risk involved with every newly opened position.

In addition, a traders should only activate new trades if you're the anticipated reward has been calculated to be at least double the maximum loss. In fact, an RR ratio of 1:3 or higher is preferable.

Consequently, traders need to know exactly where to locate stop losses and targets before new positions opened is this requirement is to be satisfied. Guidelines on how to locate stop losses and targets will now be discussed.

For instance, a trader may decide to develop a trading strategy that includes different profit targets. For example, a pre-determined target may be selected for each new position (e.g., 100 PIPs). It may also be a good idea to utilize a technique such as a trailing stop to secure profits.

After opening a FOREX account, your broker will grant access to leverage of 100:1, or possibly even higher. Consequently, very large positions may be opened with just a small deposit. However, be cautious—traders open themselves up to significant risks by trading more than they can afford to lose.

It is therefore important to accurately determine the position size of each trade in order to combat the above problem. Traders who fail to do so are in danger of overtrading. A trader's position size should always be a pre-selected percentage of total equity. As advised in Chapter 8, traders should restrict their risk exposure to a maximum of 2 percent of total equity per trade. This risk strategy provides novices with the highest chances of survival by safeguarding their total equity.

A trader's position size and stop loss will determine the risk per trade. Position size represents the size of the position that a trader intends to open and is measured in lots. Stop loss specifies the distance from the entry value that price may advance against the open position before it will be stopped out. A trader's stop loss is calculated in PIPs.

Never activate a trade without an exit strategy. Consequently, traders must always know exactly the values of their position sizes and stop losses before opening new positions. Position size can be set to remain consistent with the established 2-percent maximum risk strategy.

Imagine that a trader plans to trade the EUR/USD currency pair and a PIP equates to US$1. The position size can be determined using the following formula:

Position size = (% risk X free margin) / (PIP value X stop loss)

If no other trades open, the value of the free margin is a trader's entire equity. Assume that a trader has a balance of US$40,000. In addition, imagine that the trader selects a stop loss of 100 PIPs. The lot size that can be traded safely now needs to be a maximum of 2 percent of the trader's total equity.

Total equity: US$40,000   PIP value: US$1

Stop loss: 100 PIPs   % risk: 2 percent

Position size = (0.02 X US$40,000) / (US$1 X 100)

As such, should the trader's 8-lot trade be stopped out, a loss of US$800 will be incurred, which is equal to 2 percent of total equity.

12.6 – Win-to-Loss Ratio and Expectancy Value

All traders need a method to help determine if their trading strategies will actually turn a profit. This objective can be achieved by determining the win-to-loss ratio and the expectancy value of the strategy. The expectancy value indicates how much profit a trader can expect to gain for every dollar risked over the long haul. Any viable strategy should exhibit a positive expectancy value or the trader will simply suffer losses.

The expectancy value of a given strategy can be determined by utilizing the following equation:

Expectancy = (% win X avg win) - (% loss X avg loss),

where % win is the percentage of trades that are winners, % loss is the percentage of trades that are losers, avg win is the average size of a win and avg loss is the average size of a loss.

Suppose a trader opens 100 trades, producing 50 wins and 50 losses. The average size of the wins was US$80 while the average size of the losses was US$30. The win-to-loss ratio can then be expressed as (50/100)100 = 50 percent. The expectancy value can now be expressed as follows:

Expectancy = (0.50 X US$80) - (0.50 X US$30)

Consequently, the trader can anticipate gaining a profit of US$25.00 for every dollar risked over the long haul.

An expectancy value is a statistical gauge that increases in reliability and accuracy with larger batches of results. As such, traders are advised to utilize at least fifty trade results in its calculation to achieve a worthwhile value.

If attaining a positive expectancy value while demo trading, proceed to recalculate these values using a live account. However, if the result is negative, improvements must be made by re-testing in demo mode.

12.7 – Use a Professional Attitude

Chapter 5 promoted the benefits of developing an expert trading psychology. Any novice should action this advice fully and start aiming to achieve this objective. Fundamentally, beginners need to enhance their patience and learn specifically to concentrate on the risks involved, as opposed to potential profits, when opening new positions.

Why does patience play such an important role in FOREX trading? To answer this question, we must compare the different trading methods used by experts and novices. For example, novices seek excitement through trading a large number of positions using shorter time frames (i.e., 1 minute, 5 minutes and 15 minutes). They mistakenly think that a lot of action equates to profits.

However, the historical statistics associated with trading short time periods indicate that this is not the best method for earning profits. Indeed, important price levels such pivot points, resistance levels and support levels wane in their effectiveness as time frames become shorter. As such, beginners have a tendency to open new positions prematurely at high levels of risk. Furthermore, as discussed earlier, using trading charts in combination with very short time frames produces unreliable results. The main attributes of these types of charts, such as crossovers, are almost meaningless.

For instance, imagine that a trader has identified that the Euro is coming under stress after a fundamental analysis indicates that some of its peripheral countries are experiencing fiscal concerns. In addition, the trader has confirmed that the EUR/USD pair has dropped over the last few days. Studying trading charts in conjunction with daily time frames or higher, the trader may still clearly detect that a strong bull channel is strongly evident. In addition, using a technical indicator may confirm that no new bear trend has yet been created, despite the recent Euro weakness.

In the same situation, traders analyzing the EUR/USD trading chart in conjunction with a 15-minute time frame could have gone short because a bearish crossover was flagging them to do so. These traders may have entered a risky trade due to the fact that they are trading against the long-term trend.

Novices waste excessive quantities of time and energy pursuing high-risk trades with little real profit potential. For instance, they may open one hundred trades that result in 70 wins, gaining an average win of US$5. However, they may average US$20 for each of the 30 losses. This represents an expectancy value of -US$2.5, implying a loss of US$2.5 for every US$1 risked over the long haul. Such an outcome would be appalling and very demoralizing after so much hard work.

In contrast, FOREX experts formulate their trading decisions by utilizing the superior statistics attributed to the longer time frames, from the daily upwards. As such, they open far fewer positions than novices, but these positions are of much higher quality. For example, over the same time period experts may activate just 10 trades, producing 8 wins with an average profit of

US$100. The two losses may produce an average loss of US$50. As such, the expectancy value of their trading strategy would be US$70, implying a gain of US$70 for every US$1 spent over the long haul.

12.8 – Using a Demo Account

In Section 7.4, a number of psychological problems that novices may experience when using demo accounts were identified. However, demo accounts are extremely useful once a trader becomes proficient at using them. For example, demo accounts can be used to confirm the performance of a trading strategy without incurring any financial risks.

When using demo accounts, attempt to simulate live trading conditions as closely as possible. Traders should use the main features of their strategies, such as the RR ratio, money management and stop-loss protection. Novices who use their demo accounts haphazardly will be ill-prepared for a live trading scenario.

When demo trading, match live conditions as closely as possible in order to experience the same psychological pressures as live trading would produce. For example, beginners should try to subject themselves to trading conditions that produce the same types of emotions (i.e., greed and fear) as are generated during live trading. Without the proper effort, demo trading produces very few stressful situations and consequently will be of little use in preparing for the ordeals ahead.

Many experts advise recording the details of all demo trades as a means of focusing attention. In addition, this practice enables traders to study this data at a later data in order to identify any patterns, positive or negative, in their trading style. Novices should ask themselves the following questions when assessing their trading styles:

1. How good are my entry and exit strategies?
2. Does my strategy enable me to naturally trade with trends?

3. How well did I handle fundamental data events?
4. Could I have prevented any losses?
5. Did I succumb to emotional pressures such as fear? As a result, did I move my stop-loss positions?
6. Did price advance as I expected after opening new positions?
7. What was my largest loss?
8. Did I let my profits run in order to achieve maximum gains?

Progressing from a demo account to a live account is a very significant transition. However, the process can be smoothed out by opening a micro account (provided by most FOREX brokers), which allows for live trading risking just ten cents per PIP. Traders can then subject themselves to the real drama and psychological experiences associated with live trading at minimum risk.

Beginners must devise methods so that they can utilize demo accounts properly in order to take full advantage of the many tools and facilities that these accounts provide. For example, use demo accounts to study technical analysis and become familiar with all the features of the broker's trading platform.

Novices should take advantages of the many tools demo accounts offer by studying charts, identifying trends and using technical indicators such as supports and resistances. It is important to confirm that a prospective broker will provide you with demo account trading tools that are identical to the tools available when going live. After becoming proficient in the basic use of a demo account, further simulate live trading by using the following concepts:

1. First, choose a currency pair to trade. Novices are advised to select the EUR/USD for the reasons discussed in Section 12.3. Ensure that all tests are conducted using only this pair until confidence and a good feel for trading dynamics are developed.

2. Beginners should adhere strictly to the concepts of their trading strategies in order to test their usefulness in

identifying prime technical features such as trends and price formations (e.g., head and shoulders).

3. Novices should experiment with as many technical indicators as possible in order to detect the best fits for their strategies.

4. Only enter and exit positions if the strategy flags you to do so. Do not perform such actions purely on whims or gut feelings.

5. Novices should not cave into their emotions by moving stop losses. Instead, they should remain faithful to their initial selections as identified by their trading strategies.

6. Record all the major details of each test so they can be studied at a later time.

7. If any changes or tweaks need to be made to the strategy after testing, its performance must be reevaluated by calculating its new win-to-loss ratio and expectancy value.

Take note that without a professional attitude, demo trading will be nothing more than a complete waste of time. Following the concepts discussed in this section will result in the realistic assessment of a trading strategy and the improvement of trading abilities.

Traders should also take the opportunity while demo trading to evaluate their risk and money management strategies. Focus a considerable amount of attention on this subject because it is very important to a trader's long-term success. Furthermore, money management is a skill that is often mishandled or ignored by many novices. They tend not to concentrate on the percentage of their total equity risked per trade but rather base their stop losses on an unrealistic number of PIPs.

Indeed, this is a serious mistake that should not be carried over into live trading. Instead, traders should risk a maximum of

2 percent of their total balance per trade. Putting this important concept to use during demo trading allows novices to gain invaluable experience that will pay dividends when live trading.

Novices should aim to simulate the emotions they will feel when going live in order to confirm whether they will adhere to their money management strategies. Take note of how you felt when price started to move rapidly against your open positions. Did you panic and adjust the positions of your stop losses? Did you feel greed? Did this cause you to alter your targets at the prospect of increased profits? The point here is that utilizing a demo account properly allows novices to determine to what degree they violate their money management strategies when pressure begins to build.

As using a demo account means that a trader will not be risking real money, one's guard is often dropped and a more lackadaisical approach is adopted. Resist this tendency or the psychological pressures associated with live trading will be too much to handle. To get the most out of demo trading, use the following suggestions:

1. A default dummy balance after a demo account is opened. However, the value provided is normally unrealistic— somewhere in the region of US$50,000. If you will not be able to match such a large sum of money when going live, do not trade with it. Instead, novices should adjust this number to equate to the amount of their respective equities. This trick will better simulate future trading conditions.

2. Beginners are reminded to adhere precisely to the concepts of their trading and money management strategies when opening positions using a demo account. The more realistic the experience that can be obtained, the better prepared traders will be for the transition to live trading.

3. Again, record all results as a means of assessing compliance with both the trading and money management strategies.

If this data can also be used to identify trends in your trading style, then these experiences will help immensely when going live.

It should be appreciated that traders must contend with more intense emotions when live trading. This is because FOREX can generate significant levels of volatility that produce price spikes and surges. Consequently, this requires making serious decisions quickly and consistently in order to protect one's equity.

Under these conditions, stress levels can climb rapidly, causing traders to abandon strategies. If traders skip the all-important demo trading stage, they will not know how to handle such difficult conditions effectively. Traders should always imagine that their own money is at risk, which should then cause the adrenaline to start pumping. At this point, the prime objective is to learn how to retain composure under such pressure.

It is for this very reason that traders are advised to document their feelings during demo trading. This allows for the identification of any weaknesses at a later time. For instance, if a particular resolution isn't adequate to cope with live trading conditions, a trader may freeze and consequently be unable to make quality decisions.

Beginners are also recommended to advance their trading experience in small steps of incremental risk. Develop a testing conveyor belt of sorts comprised of historical back testing, demo testing, micro trading (10 cents per PIP), mini trading (US$1 per PIP) and full live trading (US$10 per PIP), in this order. Utilizing such an approach will allow traders to deal more easily with increasing levels of psychological and emotional stress.

12.9 – The Importance of Recording Results

Learning how to control emotions is a difficult skill to acquire when trading FOREX. Without the proper psychological preparation, live trading is guaranteed to produce stress. Novices may imagine that everything is great if they are winning. However, this is a dangerous attitude to adopt as a winning sequence can cause even the best traders to become overconfident. Of course, this results in overtrading. Additionally, greed can affect judgment, making traders interfere with their stop losses and targets. When trading FOREX, out-of-control emotions equate to financial losses because they perpetuate the following bad habits:

1. Not exiting positions in accordance with a tested trading strategy

2. Failing to allow winning trades to run

3. Not opening new positions in accordance with a tested trading strategy

4. Exposing equity to unacceptable levels of risk by overtrading

5. Not coping well with hesitation and uncertainty

6. Panicking and exiting trades prematurely

Succeeding at FOREX trading requires the psychological strength to control emotions. Many experts recommend maintaining a trading diary to assist in acquiring this mindset. It is important to record the key details of each position opened. The four main pieces of information that should be recorded in a novice's trading diary are explained below.

1. Date and Time of each position opened: This information can be used to locate a particular trade very quickly.

2. Entry and exit strategies for each position entered: This data can be used to evaluate the performance of a strategy and determine if it needs improving.

3. Description of emotions: These records can be used to detect main behavioral patterns at a later date.

4. Entry price, exit price and lot size of each trade entered: These details may be studied in order to detect possible patterns

within a trading style (i.e., whether the money management strategy is being complied with consistently or whether overtrading is occurring regularly).

In particular, here is a recommended list of details to be logged for each new position opened:

1. Date
2. Time
3. Reasons for entering the trade
4. Entry price
5. Number of lots opened
6. Protective stop value
7. Target price (if any)
8. Reasons for exiting the trade
9. Exit price
10. Emotions felt during the trade
11. Result

After acquiring a reasonably sized batch of results, this information can be studied to identify trends. Novices should ask themselves the following questions:

1. Did I move my stop during the trade?
2. Did I overtrade?
3. Did my emotions affect my trading?
4. Did the market proceed as I expected?
5. Did I need to make a drawdown?
6. Did fundamental releases affect my trading?
7. Did I trade with the trend?
8. Did I allow my profits to run?
9. Can I now improve my entry and exit criteria?
10. Could I have managed my trades better?

Traders benefit from maintaining a FOREX diary because it enables them to analyze their training data in order to identify improvements and trends. They will also be able to assess if they are constantly making the same mistakes and detect which of their trading actions are producing the best profits. For instance, many

FOREX novices constantly make the following common errors:

1. They do not understand the concepts of leverage. Many novices become over-excited when they first acquire extensive leverage facilities. This can cause them to overtrade, exposing their equities to very high levels of risk. In comparison, experts always closely follow the edicts of their money management strategies by usually restricting their risk to a maximum of 2 percent of their entire equity per trade.

2. Beginners become too dependent on technical analysis. They tend to place too much emphasis on technical analysis and technical indicators. Instead, one's chances of success may be improved if fundamental analysis is incorporated into a trading strategy.

3. Novices select poor stop losses. Stop losses must always be designed in consideration of a money management strategy. Relying on gut instincts and whims is a sure route to failure.

4. Beginners underestimate the impact that their emotions can have on their trading. Traders should always maintain a training diary as it will help to understand and better control these intangible forces.

5. Inexperienced traders do not know how to evaluate their trading strategies. If a trader uses a trading strategy without validating its performance, losses will be incurred. Section 12.6 shows how to professionally test a trading strategy by calculating the win-to-loss ratio and the expectancy value at each stage of the strategy's development.

6. Novices do not fully appreciate that FOREX is an ever-evolving entity. Strategies cannot simply be tested once and then forgotten about. Instead, the performance of a strategy must be evaluated on a regular basis by using the concepts indicated in Section 12.6.

7. Beginners have a dangerous tendency of trying to trade using shorter time frames. As they do not understand how to deal with the volatility and complexities that FOREX can produce during short time frames, they suffer serious losses.

Depending on how thorough a trader intends to be, a diary may be developed using a variety of methods, from noting thoughts and trading details in a notebook to keeping more comprehensive electronic files. Most traders opt to utilize some type of electronic storage, such as a word processor, spreadsheet or database.

Traders should store more than just trading details in their diaries. In fact, a diary should contain descriptions of all the FOREX strategies used together with any alterations to the strategies as they occur. This includes recording money management strategies together with the performance results. If this is done, all the vital data required for future analysis will be readily available in one easy to access location.

Make a point of carefully registering the emotions experienced during each open trade. For instance, which feelings were prominent and did they affect the quality of trading decisions? Also, state any mistakes that emotions may have brought about. It should also be noted whether external influences such as technical problems affected trading performance in any way.

After trading for a period of time, novices should assess the performance of their strategies by using the details of all opened positions to produce an expectancy value. This may allow for the detection of trends, which could in turn improve the performance of the strategy. For example, if any deterioration in trading performance is noticed, a recalculation of the strategy's win-to-loss ratio and expectancy value is required.

Experts use their diaries to aid in the performance of many important tasks. A well-kept diary will definitely assist novices in adopting a more disciplined and scientific approach to trading because it provides a solid foundation where the basics can be worked through in the proper manner.

All novices should attempt to develop a professional and business-like mindset as a matter of priority from the very outset. This objective can be achieved by removing emotions from trading decisions. Consequently, a trading diary can become a valuable tool in first determining the main parameters of a FOREX trading strategy and then assessing its potential for profit over the long haul.

13

Sample FOREX Strategy

Sample FOREX Strategy

Chapter 12 identified the steps required to design, test and use a viable FOREX trading strategy. This chapter provides a step-by-step guide using a real strategy that was developed in 2010.

13.1 – Time Frame

The Daily time frame was selected because the statistics generated by this time frame are very reliable and accurate. In addition, any technical indicators selected will provide very creditable advisory signals using this time frame. Traders can therefore have more confidence that their equities will be protected.

13.2 – EMA Technical Indicator

This strategy will use the EMA (9, close) and EMA (50, close) as its primary technical indicators. The following diagram demonstrates them in action using the daily time frame.

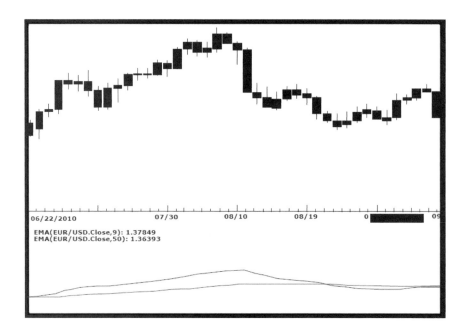

EMA(EUR/USD.Close,9): 1.37849
EMA(EUR/USD.Close,50): 1.36393

13.3 – Selecting Currency Pairs

The strategy was traded by using a number of currency pairs in order to optimize its chances of identifying profitable trades. In particular, all the major pairs were included (i.e., EUR/USD, USD/YEN, GBP/USD, USD/CHF, USD/CAD, AUD/EUR and NZD/USD). A number of other pairs that possessed low spreads were also involved.

However, novices should heed the advice outlined in Chapter 12. Specifically, they should initially base their strategies on trading only the EUR/USD currency pair because they will then be able to benefit from its constant high liquidity and low spreads. They will also be able to access significant advice about any new trading opportunities because almost 80% of all FOREX transactions involve the EUR/USD.

Always remember that the EUR/USD pair displays spreads that usually never exceed 3 PIPs. In addition, traders will hardly ever experience any problems opening new EUR/USD positions because of its high liquidity.

13.4 – Confirmation Strategy Using Pivot Points

This strategy will use pivot points, as well as support and resistance levels to act as its confirmation tool. As these levels will be produced on daily time frame charts, they will provide very strong indications that price has the potential to proceed further in its current direction. A number of examples are discussed in the next section.

As advised in Section 12.4, traders must take these extra measures to safeguard their equities from significant price reversals, retractions and fakeouts. Very importantly, this step should not be overlooked because it provides the increased confidence of knowing that new positions will have the maximum potential to succeed. Chapters 6 and 11 have provided the descriptions of a number of excellent technical indicators. In addition, those new to designing FOREX trading strategies may find that the candlestick indicator described in Section 10.2 is of great help.

13.5 – Entry and Exit Conditions

This strategy will employ the following entry and exit rules for opening and closing trading positions:

1. Buy positions will only be entered when price is in a bull trend, which can be confirmed by detecting that the EMA9 is above the EMA50.
2. Under bullish conditions, a new position should be opened once price has first broken through R1 and then gained an additional 20 PIPs.
3. The position should be closed once price has touched R2.
4. Sell positions must only be entered when price is in a bear trend, which can be confirmed by detecting that EMA9 is below EMA50.
5. Under bearish conditions, a new position should be opened once price has first broken below S1 and then achieved an additional 20 PIPs.

6. The position should be closed after price reaches S2.
7. Only a maximum of 2 percent of equity per trade will be traded, as will be explained in more detail in the next section.

Example 1

On the following EUR/AUD chart, the EMA9 is lower than the EMA50, which implies that only sell positions may be opened. Such a trade was activated on August 20th.2010 after price penetrated the S1 level at 1.4263 by a further 20 PIPs. On August 23rd, 2010, the position was closed after price achieved S2, realizing a profit. This result can be verified by inspecting the account results presented at the end of this section. Find the trade information between the August 20th and 23rd and note that the strategy was tested using a micro account.

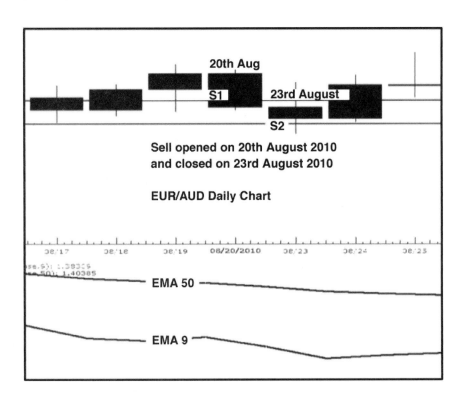

Example 2

In the next example, price is in a bearish trend because EMA9 is below EMA50 on the USD/CHF daily trading chart. A new sell position was opened on August 26th, 2010 after price dropped below S1 at 1.0259 by a further 20 PIPs. On August 31st, 2010, the trade was terminated after price touched S2 located at 1.0192, resulting in a profit. The details of this trade may again be studied by looking at the end of this section and inspecting the data generated between August 26th and 31st.

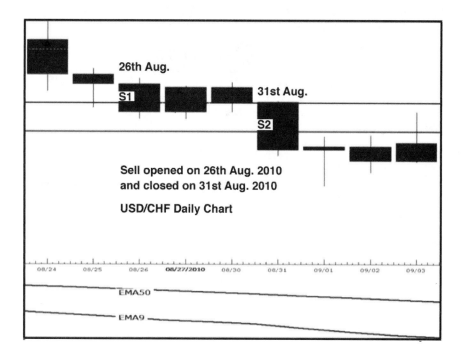

Example 3

Once again, a bearish trend, with EMA9 well below EMA50 on the USD/YEN daily trading chart, can be seen. A new sell position was opened September 14th, 2010 after price plunged below S1 at 83.40 by an additional 20 PIPs. This trade was closed on the same day after price touched S2 located at 82.96, realizing another profit. This trade's details may be checked by visiting the account results located at the end of this section and inspecting the data produced on September 14th, 2010.

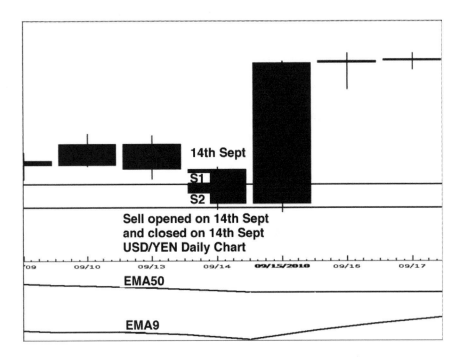

14th Sept

S1

S2

**Sell opened on 14th Sept
and closed on 14th Sept
USD/YEN Daily Chart**

EMA50

EMA9

Example 4

In this example, a bullish trend is prominent with EMA9 well above EMA50 on the NZD/USD daily trading chart. A new buy position was opened on September 22nd, 2010 after price surged above R1 at 0.7364 by an additional 20 PIPs. This trade was then terminated on the same day after price touched S2 located at 0.7403, producing a profit. This trade's details using the method described in the previous three examples.

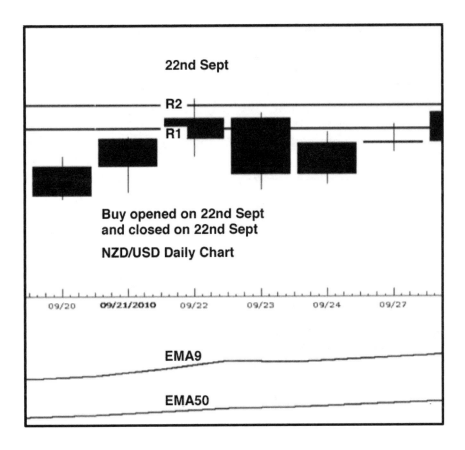

22nd Sept

R2

R1

Buy opened on 22nd Sept
and closed on 22nd Sept

NZD/USD Daily Chart

09/20   09/21/2010   09/22   09/23   09/24   09/27

EMA9

EMA50

13.6 – Risk Strategy

Chapter 8 and Section 12.5 have already discussed developing a risk strategy in some depth. Basically, traders must have an exit strategy for every position that they open. This requirement implies always knowing precisely the size of one's position and stop loss even before activating any new trades.

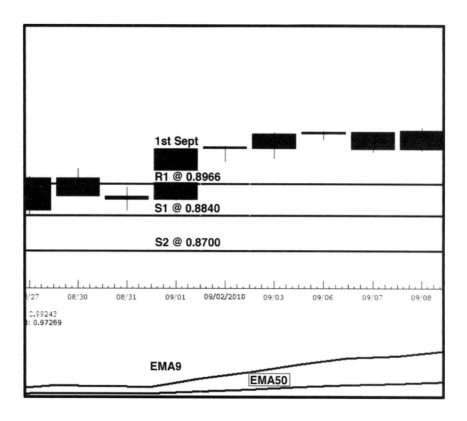

This strategy risked a maximum of 2 percent of entire equity per trade. These two parameters can be calculated so that they comply to any risk strategy as follows: Assume a trader's equity equals US$50,000 and each 1-PIP movement is worth US$1. In the above diagram, the blue bull candle on September 1st, 2010 surged above R1 by an additional 20 PIPs, opening a new position at 0.8986.

The position size must now be calculated so that a maximum

of 2 percent of total equity is risked. The above diagram presents two of the many possible choices that can be made, depending on one's trading personality.

1. Aggressive Traders

A trader may opt to locate a stop loss below S1 by a distance of 24 PIPs. As such, position size can now be calculated by using the following formula:

Position size = (% risk X free margin) / (PIP value X stop loss)

Assume no other trades are open at present. Consequently, the free margin will equate to the trader's entire equity (i.e., US$50,000). In addition, the size of the stop loss equals 0.8986 minus 0.8816, or 170 PIPs.

Account balance: US$50,000   PIP value: US$1

Stop loss: 170 PIPs   % risk: 2%

Position size = (0.02 X US$50,000) / (US$1 X 170)

As can be seen above, the position size is 5 lots, rounded down to the nearest whole figure in order to ensure the new trade complies with the risk strategy.

Consequently, if the 5-lot position were stopped out, then a loss of 5 X US$1 X 170 would be incurred, equaling a total loss of US$850, which complies with the maximum risk strategy established.

2. Defensive Traders

Defensive traders may position their stop losses below S2 by 24 PIPs. Position size can now be determined using the following parameters:

Account balance: US$50,000   PIP value: US$1

Stop loss: 310 PIPs   % risk: 2%

Position size = (% risk X free margin) / (PIP value X stop loss)

Position size = (0.02 X US$50,000) / (US$1 X 310)

As can be seen above, the position size is 3 lots. Consequently, if the 3-lot position were stopped out, a loss of 3 X US$1 X 310 would be incurred, equaling a total loss of US$910, which satisfies the maximum risk strategy established.

Special Note

Until a good understanding of how to trade FOREX is

TABLE 1

Symbol	Volume	Date/Time	Sold	Bought	Gross P/L
EUR/JPY	3,000	7/21/2010 13:10	111.1		
		7/21/2010 19:39		110.531	19.7
EUR/JPY	2,000	7/21/2010 19:54	110.391		
		7/22/2010 1:12		110.207	4.26
EUR/JPY	1,000	7/22/2010 1:37	110.007		
		8/11/2010 4:54		110.822	-11.66
EUR/USD	3,000	7/27/2010 6:22		1.30279	
		7/27/2010 6:52	1.30402		3.69
AUD/USD	3,000	7/27/2010 6:56		0.90685	
		8/1/2010 19:17	0.9085		4.95
EUR/CHF	2,000	7/27/2010 11:16		1.37932	
		8/4/2010 9:45	1.38148		4.11
EUR/USD	1,000	7/29/2010 4:11		1.30682	
		7/29/2010 4:31	1.30764		0.82
USD/CAD	1,000	7/29/2010 5:01	1.03084		
		7/30/2010 11:18		1.02674	3.99
GBP/USD	1,000	7/29/2010 5:02		1.56631	
		7/30/2010 10:36	1.56975		3.44
USD/JPY	1,000	7/29/2010 5:59	86.807		
		7/29/2010 11:05		86.74	0.77
USD/JPY	1,000	7/30/2010 2:43	86.221		
		7/30/2010 7:40		85.98	2.8

AUD/USD	3,000	8/1/2010 20:17		0.9106	
		8/2/2010 2:55	0.9126		6
NZD/USD	1,000	8/2/2010 2:21		0.73078	
		8/2/2010 2:41	0.73151		0.73
GBP/USD	1,000	8/2/2010 2:27		1.57836	
		8/2/2010 5:36	1.58183		3.47
EUR/AUD	3,000	8/2/2010 2:55	1.43147		
		8/11/2010 11:10		1.43145	0.05
EUR/USD	1,000	8/2/2010 7:53		1.31027	
		8/2/2010 8:19	1.31162		1.35
EUR/USD	1,000	8/2/2010 8:45		1.31446	
		8/2/2010 9:08	1.31498		0.52
USD/CAD	1,000	8/2/2010 9:09	1.02121		
		8/4/2010 10:17		1.01914	2.03
EUR/USD	1,000	8/3/2010 5:04		1.32543	
		8/6/2010 8:47	1.32941		3.98
AUD/USD	1,000	8/4/2010 7:29		0.91771	
		8/6/2010 8:46	0.92071		3
USD/CAD	1,000	8/5/2010 5:01	1.01185		
		9/14/2010 9:46		1.02379	-11.66
USD/JPY	1,000	8/6/2010 7:31	85.471		
		8/6/2010 7:39		85.239	2.72
USD/CHF	1,000	8/6/2010 7:56	1.03851		
		8/6/2010 9:16		1.0342	4.17
GBP/USD	1,000	8/6/2010 7:56		1.59461	
		8/6/2010 9:01	1.59815		3.54
GBP/USD	1,000	8/6/2010 9:05	1.5983		
		8/6/2010 9:10		1.59865	-0.35
GBP/USD	1,000	8/6/2010 9:05	1.59927		
		8/6/2010 9:10		1.59865	0.62
GBP/USD	1,000	8/6/2010 9:07	1.59895		
		8/6/2010 9:10		1.59865	0.3
EUR/CHF	2,000	8/9/2010 10:27		1.38592	
		8/10/2010 7:20	1.38817		4.25
USD/JPY	2,000	8/10/2010 13:17	85.604		
		8/10/2010 16:01		85.455	3.49
USD/JPY	2,000	8/10/2010 18:18	85.332		
		8/11/2010 3:02		85.029	7.13
EUR/JPY	2,000	8/11/2010 1:12	111.614		
		8/11/2010 4:54		110.822	18.62

USD/JPY	3,000	8/11/2010 6:05	84.863		
		8/19/2010 9:08		85.037	-6.14
EUR/AUD	2,000	8/11/2010 8:14	1.43591		
		8/11/2010 11:10		1.43145	8.04
EUR/JPY	2,000	8/11/2010 17:39	109.261		
		8/19/2010 18:21		109.263	-0.05
USD/JPY	2,000	8/11/2010 17:40	85.145		
		8/19/2010 9:08		85.037	2.54
EUR/CHF	2,000	8/12/2010 6:39	1.35377		
		8/12/2010 14:28		1.34685	13.19
USD/CHF	1,000	8/12/2010 8:41	1.0501		
		8/12/2010 14:30		1.04952	0.55
EUR/AUD	2,000	8/13/2010 0:38	1.4259		
		8/13/2010 9:24		1.4234	4.49
AUD/USD	1,000	8/13/2010 0:40		0.90271	
		8/17/2010 3:39	0.903		0.29
NZD/USD	1,000	8/13/2010 0:40		0.71655	
		8/18/2010 5:08	0.71654		-0.01
EUR/CHF	1,000	8/15/2010 16:38	1.33738		
		8/16/2010 2:54		1.334	3.25
USD/CHF	1,000	8/15/2010 16:48	1.04755		
		8/16/2010 1:39		1.04497	2.47
GBP/USD	1,000	8/16/2010 9:19		1.56832	
		9/15/2010 9:59	1.56321		-5.11
EUR/USD	1,000	8/17/2010 3:24		1.28975	
		9/3/2010 14:48	1.28915		-0.6
AUD/USD	1,000	8/17/2010 10:03		0.9048	
		8/17/2010 10:42	0.90722		2.42
NZD/USD	1,000	8/17/2010 10:37		0.71366	
		8/18/2010 5:08	0.71654		2.88
EUR/AUD	1,000	8/17/2010 10:38	1.4201		
		8/23/2010 5:46		1.41768	2.17
NZD/USD	1,000	8/18/2010 7:17		0.71892	
		8/29/2010 17:18	0.71301		-5.91
EUR/CHF	1,000	8/19/2010 2:58	1.334		
		8/19/2010 3:21		1.33135	2.55
USD/CHF	1,000	8/19/2010 7:31	1.03725		
		8/19/2010 7:37		1.03495	2.22
EUR/JPY	2,000	8/19/2010 9:37	109.333		
		8/19/2010 18:21		109.263	1.64
EUR/JPY	4,000	8/20/2010 3:56	108.958		
		8/20/2010 4:55		108.64	14.89
EUR/CHF	4,000	8/20/2010 5:24	1.31429		
		8/23/2010 1:41		1.3113	11.61
EUR/AUD	2,000	8/20/2010 13:46	1.42435		
		8/23/2010 5:46		1.41768	11.96

developed, always use the more defensive risk strategy (i.e., the second of the two above examples). This is because FOREX can generate very high levels of volatility that can easily stop out overleveraged positions.

13.7 – How Good is Your Strategy?

This question of how useful a strategy is can be answered by calculating the win-to-loss ratio and the expectancy value of the strategy as described in Section 12.6. The win-to-loss ratio and expectancy value of the trading strategy introduced in this chapter will now be determined using the following equations:

Win-to-loss ratio = (Number of wins / Total number of trades)100

Expectancy = (% win X avg win) - (% loss X avg loss)

The table located at the end of this section shows the results that this trading strategy achieved from late July to the end of August 2010. The main parameters recorded were as follows:

Total number of trades: 54
Total number of wins: 46
Total number of losses: 8
Total value of wins: US$210.06
Total value of losses: US$40.89

Using these figures, the following parameters were also determined:

Average win: US$4.56
Average loss: US$5.11
Win-to-loss ratio: 85%
Expectancy: US$3.11

As such, this strategy can be expected to realize a US$3.11 profit for every dollar risked over the long haul.

13.8 – Trading Professionally

Section 12.7 explained the benefits of achieving an expert psychology to aid in trading FOREX. This trading strategy was used to constantly attain realistic targets. Patience was consistently practiced throughout this process. In fact, the strategy itself encouraged such an approach as it was based on the daily time frame.

The results in the above table confirm that important indicators such as pivot points, resistance levels and support levels were far more effective because a longer time frame was used. From examining the above table is should also be clear that new positions were carefully selected so that the maximum risk per trade was compliant with the selected risk and money management strategy.

This strategy did not make its user expend excessive quantities of time and energy in pursuing trades that exhibited little real profit potential. Instead, positions were only activated after making decisions based on the superior statistics attributed to the daily time frame. Consequently, although fewer positions were opened, they were of high quality.

13.9 – Strategy Evaluation

This trading strategy was applied throughout by consistently adhering to the concepts defined for its RR ratio, money management strategy, stop-loss protection, etc. The key parameters for each test were recorded and later analyzed, producing the following conclusions about the strategy's performance:

1. The entry and exit strategies used were effective but could be improved.
2. This strategy was designed to trade trends and was successful at doing so.
3. The strategy needs to be improved in order to be able to better cope with fundamental data events.
4. Although the strategy minimized losses, its design could

be improved to capture better profits.

5. It was traded successfully without involving any human emotions.

6. The strategy achieved a good record at predicting the correct price direction.

7. Table 1 in Section 13.7 shows the largest loss.

8. Profits were recorded in accordance with the exit strategy used.

The strategy was traded using a micro account in order to restrict losses and reduce psychological problems. A professional attitude was adopted during the entire period during which the strategy was live traded. This meant that decisions were always based on the risk strategy and not influenced by gut instincts.

Furthermore, at no time was a stop loss moved when price started to move against a position. Additionally, targets were not adjusted in order to achieve greater levels of profits. The strategy was allowed to operate entirely on its own without any user interference.

Although there is definitely room for improvement, the strategy was allowed to deal with FOREX volatility completely on its own and performed reasonably well. Consequently, the users did not suffer any form of stress as they were not directly involved in the trading process.

13.10 – Recording Emotions

While trading this strategy, all emotions were recorded and the following conclusions were derived after analyzing the data:

1. All positions were closed when users were flagged to do so.

2. Profits were taken in accordance with the strategy's design.

3. All new positions were opened when users were advised to do so.

4. Equity was never overtraded and was exposed to a maximum risk of only 2 percent of total equity.

5. The effects of human emotions were minimized during the trading process.
6. No trades were exited prematurely for any reason.

The details of each trade were recorded in accordance with the recommendations stated in Section 12.9. After studying the information, the following conclusions were derived:

1. No stop-losses were moved during active trading.
2. Equity was not subjected to overtrading.
3. All human emotions were minimized.
4. The strategy achieved a good record of predicting future price movements, although room for improvement certainly exists.
5. No excessive drawdowns were made
6. The strategy handled fundamental events reasonably well, although improvement is need with regard to this aspect of trading.
7. The strategy traded long-term trends well.
8. Profits were secured in accordance with the exit strategy.
9. Results indicate that both the entry and exit strategies could be improved.
10. The design of the strategy should be reassessed to achieve an improved expectancy value.

The strategy was shown to cope with leverage very well and did not experience any serious problems in this area. However, it did tend to lean too much toward technical analysis at the expense of fundamental analysis. In summary, a successful attempt was made to trade the strategy using a professional and business-like mindset by minimizing emotions from all trading decisions. However, a reassessment of the strategy's performance needs to be performed as there is always room for improvement.

14

Summary

Glossary

Ask   The selling price of a currency pair

Aussie   The nickname for the AUD/USD currency pair

Candlesticks   A famous methodology for representing the daily trading price range (open, high, low and close)

Carry   The cost incurred for maintaining a pair active from one day to the next

Base currency   The first currency quoted in a pair; the Euro is the base currency in the EUR/USD pair

Bear market   A time period during which the value of currency pairs continuously declines

Bear   A trader who is of the opinion that the values of particular currency pairs will fall

Bid   The buying price of a currency pair

Bid/Ask spread   The PIP difference between the ask value and bid value of a currency pair

Broker   An agent used to action orders such as the buying and selling of currency pairs

Bull A trader who is of the opinion that the values of particular currency pairs will rise

Bull market A time period during which the value of a currency pair will continuously appreciate

Correlation A statistical term that represents a relationship between two currency pairs

Currency pair Two currencies that are traded against each other

Day trader A trader who attempts to undertake short-term price movements for profit

Drawdown The reduction in equity produced by a losing FOREX trade

ECN broker Provides traders access to an electronic FOREX trading network

Equity Net worth equaling total assets minus total liabilities

Exotics Lesser known and traded currency pairs

Foreign exchange Used to buy and sell currency pairs

Fundamental analysis The study of economic factors that affect the values of currency pairs

Fundamental trader An investor who favors using fundamental analysis Head and shoulders A price pattern that exhibits three peaks; the middle peak is higher than the surrounding shoulders on either side

218

Hedge — The action of reducing risk by utilizing two counterbalancing currency pairs

Interday trading — Positions that are entered and exited within the same trading day

Liquidity — The active volume of active traders who are buying and selling currency pairs

Long — When a trader buys the first currency in the pair

Lots — Term representing 100,000 units of a particular currency.

Margin — The minimum deposit required to keep a currency pair position open

Margin call — A notification produced by a broker informing traders that more funds are required in order to keep their positions open

Market order — An order to open a new trading position immediately at the best currency price

Mini account — Allows traders to operate using smaller lot sizes

Overbought — Occurs after the price of a currency rises to an abnormally high value after climbing in value more quickly than its usual trading patterns

Oversold — Occurs after the price of a currency drops to an abnormally low value after falling in value more quickly than its usual trading patterns

PIP — The smallest price movements used in FOREX trading

Profit taking — Exiting a position to secure a profit

Quantitative easing — A practice used by central banks to stimulate spending within an economy

Quote currency — The second currency of a currency pair (for instance, the USD is the quote currency in the EUR/USD)

Resistance — Price level at which a currency pair is anticipated to sell off

Risk management — A strategy used to reduce financial risk

Short — When a trader buys the second currency in a currency pair

Spike — An abnormally rapid movement in price

Spread — The difference or variance between the ask value and the bid value of a currency pair

Stochastic oscillator — A famous technical indicator

Stop losses — A pre-set position at which a position will be closed in order to control and restrict financial losses

Technical analysis — An attempt to predict the price movements of currency pairs by studying market data such as historical price trends.

Technical indicators — Tools used to track and predict the movements in the values of currency pairs

Technical trader   A trader who prefers using technical analysis

Trading platforms   Sophisticated software applications used to trade FOREX, usually via the internet

Trend   The current directions of currency pairs.

Trend lines   Line that are displayed on trading charts to help predict the future directions of currency pairs

Volatility   The size in fluctuation that the value of a currency pair can achieve during a predetermined time period

References

Ref No.   Reference Description

1   Foreign exchange market - http://en.wikipedia.org/wiki/Foreign_
exchange_market

2   Major currencies - http://www.businessdictionary.com/definition/
major-currencies.html

3   Leverage (finance) - http://en.wikipedia.org/wiki/Leverage_
(finance)

4   Interbank Market - http://www.investopedia.com/terms/i/
interbankmarket.asp

5   Risk Aversion - http://financecareers.about.com/od/rz/g/Risk_
Aversion.htm

6   Economic Calendar - http://www.bloomberg.com/markets/
economic-calendar/

7   Market Maker - http://beginnersinvest.about.com/od/
beginnerscorner/l/blmarketmakers.htm

8   Electronic Communication Network – http://www.investopedia.
com/terms/e/ecn.asp

9   What is a Forex spread? - http://forextrading.about.com/od/
forexfaqs/f/spread.htm

10   Forex Broker - http://www.forextraders.com/forex-broker-reviews.
html

11   Money Management - http://www.swing-trade-stocks.com/
money-management.html

12   Volatility - http://forextrading.about.com/od/advancedtrading/a/
forex_volatile.htm

13   Technical analysis - http://en.wikipedia.org/wiki/Technical_analysis

14   Expectancy Value - http://hubpages.com/hub/Your-own-Forex-
Trading-System---Part-23

15   Forex Liquidity - http://financial-dictionary.thefreedictionary.com/
liquidity

16   Fundamental Analysis - http://www.investopedia.com/terms/f/
fundamentalanalysis.asp

17   Dow Jones Index - http://en.wikipedia.org/wiki/Dow_Jones_
Industrial_Average

18   SMA Indicator - http://investor.sacc.com/Moving-Average-

Indicator.cfm

19   EMA - http://stockcharts.com/school/doku.php?id=chart_school:technical_indicators:moving_averages

20   RSI - http://en.wikipedia.org/wiki/Relative_Strength_Index

21   Stochastic - http://stockcharts.com/school/doku.php?id=chart_school:technical_indicators:stochastic_oscillator

22   Risk-to-Reward ratio - http://www.simple-stock-trading.com/riskrewardratio.html

23   Margin Calls - http://daytrading.about.com/od/mtoo/g/MarginCall.htm

24   Candlesticks - http://stockcharts.com/school/doku.php?id=chart_school:chart_analysis:introduction_to_candlesticks

25   Bar Charts - http://www.forexrealm.com/technical-analysis/technical-charts/bar-chart.html

26   Carry Trade - http://www.investopedia.com/terms/c/currencycarrytrade.asp

27   Fibonacci retracements - http://www.onlinetradingconcepts.com/TechnicalAnalysis/Fibonacci.html

28   Bollinger Bands - http://www.bollingeronbollingerbands.com/

29   Elliot Wave Oscillator - http://www.tradingfives.com/articles/elliott_oscillator.htm

30   Commodity Channel Index - http://www.incrediblecharts.com/indicators/commodity_channel_index.php

31   DeMarker Indicator - http://www.babypips.com/forexpedia/DeMarker_Indicator

32   Money Flow Index - http://en.wikipedia.org/wiki/Money_Flow_Index

33   On Balance Volume - http://www.incrediblecharts.com/indicators/on_balance_volume.php

34   DMI - http://stockcharts.com/help/doku.php?id=chart_school:technical_indicators:average_directional_

35   True Strength Index - http://www.investopedia.com/terms/t/tsi.asp

36   Pivot points - http://en.wikipedia.org/wiki/Pivot_point

Index